THE LIFE OF
SAINT FRANCIS OF ASSISI

THE LIFE
OF
SAINT FRANCIS
OF ASSISI

E. E. REYNOLDS

Including
The Way of Life of the Secular Franciscan Order
and
Meditations on the Franciscan Vocation

ANTHONY CLARKE
WHEATHAMPSTEAD, HERTFORDSHIRE

First published in Great Britain in 1983 by
ANTHONY CLARKE BOOKS, Wheathampstead
Hertfordshire, England.

USA edition: CHRISTIAN CLASSICS, Westminster, Maryland 1983

Acknowledgements: Notes on the Secular Franciscan
Order and The New Rule used by permission of The
Franciscan Friary, Forest Gate, London.
One Thing More, Meditations; used by permission of
© The Society of Saint Francis, Brookfield, Queensland,
Australia

(UK edition) ISBN 085650 061 5
(USA edition) ISBN 0 87061 081 3

Made and printed in Great Britain by
Robert Hartnoll Ltd. Bodmin, Cornwall

Contents

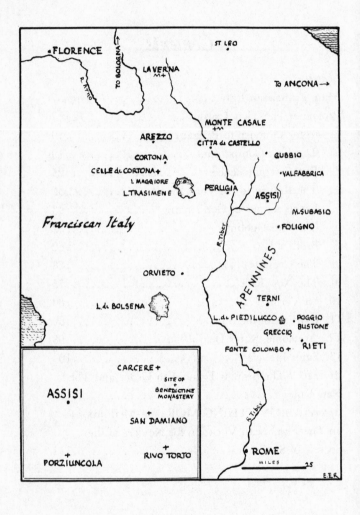

Franciscan Italy

FLORENCE

TO BOLOGNA →

LA VERNA
M+

ST LEO

To ANCONA →

MONTE CASALE
+M

AREZZO

CITTA di CASTELLO

GUBBIO

CORTONA

CELLE di CORTONA +

L. MAGGIORE

L. TRASIMENE

PERUGIA

VALFABBRICA

ASSISI

M. SUBASIO

FOLIGNO

ORVIETO •

R. TIBER

APENNINES

TERNI

L. di BOLSENA

L. di PIEDILUCCO

POGGIO
BUSTONE

GRECCIO

RIETI

FONTE COLOMBO +

CARCERE +

SITE OF
BENEDICTINE
MONASTERY

ASSISI

+
SAN DAMIANO

+
PORZIUNCOLA

+
RIVO TORTO

R. TIBER

ROME

MILES   25

E.E.R

Prologue
The Two Tramps

IT was my last day in Assisi. For some years I had been
familiar with the early Franciscan records (in the five
small volumes in the Temple Classics series) and with two or
three modern biographies. My visit was indeed a pilgrimage.
I was prepared for the contrast between the poverty of the
saint and the magnificence of the basilica that entombs him,
but the first sight of that vast structure, thrusting itself over
the plain like a monstrous battleship, proved more
dumbfounding than I had foreseen. Throughout my stay this
glaring incongruity oppressed me. I felt that there was always
something between me and Saint Francis. I could not reach
him. I understood the desire of his successors and of the great
multitude of his followers to pay their tribute by visible tokens
in buildings and paintings. I spent hours studying the frescoes
in the Upper and Lower Churches and I sensed how much
would be lost if they had not been painted, yet .... It was
therefore with a feeling of frustration that I went down to the
crypt to make my farewell prayers. I knelt on the bottom step
leading up to the altar that stands below the tomb of the saint.
Presently I was aware that others had joined me, one on my
right and one on my left. When I got up, I saw that they were
two tramps, unkempt and in rags. Had I met them in a by-
lane I should have been glad to get past them safely. I
remained near the door until they came out. They looked at
complete peace with the world. No doubt out in the blinding
sunshine they would soon be up to some skulduggery again
but at least they had had their moment of stillness and of

comfort. So, almost at the last hour I knew that I had at last found Saint Francis in his own Assisi.

Nearly a quarter of a century has passed and, whenever my thoughts turn to the saint, it is not to the basilica, nor even to the Porziuncola but to those two tramps on their knees before the tomb of Il Poverello.

E.E.R.

1.

From Affluence to Beggary

SAINT Francis was born at Assisi in 1181 or 1182. His father Pietro Bernardone, was a prosperous cloth-merchant who had a trading connection with Provence. He was away in France when his eldest son was born. The mother had the boy christened Giovanni, but, on his return, her husband nicknamed him Francesco, perhaps to record a profitable business journey. It is not necessary to presume that the mother was of Provençal origin; she may have been, but this is conjectural. The name stuck and was to become one of the popular Christian names, though there are some rare instances of its earlier use.

Nothing is known of his boyhood. He could read and write, and learned some Latin, but he was not scholarly inclined.

The little town of Assisi stands on a ledge of the Apennines and faces westwards. It is about ninety miles north of Rome and the same distance south-east of Florence, but its most formidable neighbour is Perugia, some twelve miles to the north-west. The rivalry between the two towns was immemorial and, in the twelfth century, struggles between Popes and Emperors, Guelphs and Ghibellines, led to clashes between them in petty warfare. It was at this period that the Italian cities were developing into communes, each striving to bring neighbouring towns under its rule. Within the cities there were rival groups of noble families, but the rapid expansion of trade meant the growing influence of merchants and bankers. The end of the century also saw the third and fourth abortive and discreditable crusades. It is against this background of rivalry and strife that we must see the life of Francis Bernadone.

He first comes into notice during one of the skirmishes between Assisi and Perugia; this was in 1202 when he was about twenty years of age. His father, perhaps too indulgently, allowed Francis to spend freely on rich clothes and on the trappings so essential for a young man wanting to cut a dash and be in the swim. He was accepted by the sons of the nobility not only for his generous entertainment of them, but for his gay and companionable nature. When they set out to face the Perugians, Francis was among the mounted knights as he could afford to provide his own horse and armour. The Assisians were defeated and many, including Francis, were taken to Perugia as prisoners. Francis's irrepressible good humour at first annoyed his fellow prisoners but, eventually, he put new life into them and even brought them to be on friendly terms with one of their number whom, for some offence, they had ostracized.

Francis longed to win renown for himself as a valiant knight and his father may have encouraged him in the hope that his son would raise the social position of the Bernardones. Not that trade was to be neglected and Francis had to take an active part in the cloth business which he would inherit; the earliest biographer called him 'a shrewd trader', and it was doubtless in the interests of the business that he learned French.

He seems to have returned home before the peace negotiations were concluded; perhaps his father had ransomed him, or a collapse in health may have led to his early release, for, when he got back home he was prostrated by a fever — a vague enough term in those days to cover a variety of illnesses. This physical prostration may have had lasting consequences as he was never again as robust as he had been as a youth. While he lay in bed his thoughts were driven inwards and he began to reflect on the problem of what he was to do with his life. There is a parallel here with the experience three hundred years later of the founder of another influential order, Ignatius of Loyola, who, during a long recovery from war wounds, asked for books to read, but the only one available was a volume of the lives of the saints and it was through meditating on these that Ignatius was led to a change of life. Nothing is recorded of Francis' reading; indeed, the impression is that he owed little to books. His meditations however disturbed him greatly. When he was well enough, he tottered to one of the gates of Assisi and was distressed that the sights of the countryside gave him little delight; this to one who was an open-air man was a shock.

When his strength at last returned, he plunged again into the gay life he had enjoyed before his imprisonment. Then came a new opportunity to the pursuit of knighthood. The Pope was at war in Apulia in South Italy and a Count Gentile called for volunteers to go under his command to the support of the papal forces. Francis responded at once and equipped himself with the richest armour and finest weapons, but, just before setting out, he noticed one knight was poorly supplied, so he gave him his cloak and arms and then got others for himself. His father must have doted on his son and did not question his spending. During the night before leaving Assisi, Francis dreamt that he was led into a palace that was full of the richest armour and finest weapons; he took this to mean that his knightly ambition would be attained. So he set off with his companions; their first stop was at Spoleto and here he had another dream. He heard a voice asking him whether he meant to go farther with the troop; when he replied that such was his intention, he heard the question, 'Who can do better for you, the lord or the servant?' Francis at once said, 'The Lord'; to which the voice said, 'Why then do you leave the lord for the servant and a rich lord for a poor one?' 'What do you wish me to do?' Then came the command, 'Return to Assisi and you will learn there what you must do, for it behoves you to find another meaning in your earlier dream.' These enigmatic sayings puzzled Francis, as indeed, they perplex us. They must have echoed doubts that had been forming in his mind and that had temporarily been suppressed in the excitement of this new knightly venture. So he returned to Assisi.

We are not told how this sudden change was received by his fellow soldiers, or by his father, or by the citizens, but he quickly resumed his old ways. His companions chose him as the master of their revels and he gave them a sumptuous banquet, but they noticed something strange in him; he would become lost in thought and oblivious of the roisterers around him. They had a ready explanation — Francis was in love! When they chaffed him, he replied, 'I have thoughts of taking a bride who is nobler and richer and more beautiful than any you have seen.' At this they mocked him. Was he thinking of marriage to the Church or was he already being drawn to Lady Poverty? This would, at that stage, have been little more than the shadow of a shade. What is clear is that he was in a state of spiritual uncertainty; he had glimmerings of the truth but he could not yet see where these would lead him.

We should notice that Francis did not experience a sudden, dramatic conversion; he did not share Saint Paul's experience on the road to Damascus. He moved, as we shall see, step by step, and, at first, no doubt with reluctance; his spiritual progress was lifelong. The chronology is uncertain,but it seems that two or three years elapsed between the first intimations and the final surrender.

This agonizing search for an answer to the question 'What does God want of me?' is not recorded in detail. The next incident shows that Francis was still torn between two ways of life. He decided to seek guidance at the tombs of the Apostles in Rome and joined a pilgrimage. Wearing his splendid clothes, he entered St Peter's. He was shocked to see how small were the offerings made by the well-to-do pilgrims, and, in revulsion, he threw into the treasury a handful of money; the sound of its fall startled those who had been so niggardly in their own oblations. This action may be seen as the last display of wealth by Francis. His own impulsive action may have shocked himself. Did he think of the widow's mite? The sight of the swarm of beggars round the doors of the basilica, prompted him to share their misery. What was it like to depend on the charity of passers-by? He borrowed the rags of one of them and took his place as a beggar and made his appeals in broken French. After this humiliating experience, he resumed his own clothes and returned to Assisi.

He had always been generous to the poor but when he got home again he became even more responsive to their needs; he would give away his clothes and other possessions to those who appealed to his charity. He would also secretly send chalices and vestments to poor priests. During his father's absences he would feed the poor from the household table; to this his mother made no objection, for, it is said, she loved him 'beyond her other sons.' The name of only one of them is known, Angelo, who scoffed at his brother's behaviour. There is no mention of a sister. The fact that this feeding of the poor was only done when the father was absent, suggests that Pietro had little sympathy with his eldest son's charitable work.

Francis withdrew frequently for prayer and meditation. He confided his spiritual anguish to one friend only whose name is not known. The two would go out into the countryside and, while Francis retired into a cave or into one of the old Etruscan tombs, the friend would wait for him at a distance. Here it may be noted that Francis was not by nature a solitary; he never lost his need for companionship. Even at the time of his supreme agony, the stigmatization, he craved to have near him, though out of sight, two or three of his dearest followers. He did not reveal the nature of his spiritual wrestling to this friend but one element must have been his need to abase his pride. He had relished his command of wealth, his rich clothes and the lavish banquets he could give, his prestige as the leader of the young bloods of Assisi, his ambition to display a valour that would make him a knight, even his liberality with his father's money in so readily helping the poor and distressed — the inner voice must have been warning him that all these manifestations of pride would have to be sacrificed if he chose to follow Christ. The young man who had great possessions and asked for Christ's guidance must have come to Francis's mind; was he too to go away sorrowful?

At last a clear intimation came to him of the Divine Will. He must give up all the pleasures of his past; there must be a complete renunciation. With it came the complementary need for positive action for it was part of his nature to turn thought into deed. Among his fears was that of physical contact with lepers, a fear he shared with all healthy people. So it came about that when he next rode out of Assisi and met a leper he not only gave him money but kissed his hand. Then he visited the lazar-house and gave generously to the wretched creatures who languished there, and he so far overcame his queasiness that he tended them. In later years he recalled this momentous stage in his spiritual progress;

> 'The Lord Himself gave to me, Brother Francis, thus to begin to do penance … The Lord Himself led me among the lepers, and I showed mercy to them; and, when I left them, what had seemed bitter to me was changed into sweetness of body and soul.'

Then one day as he was passing the chapel of San Damiano, he felt impelled to go in. It was a dilapidated building like a tumbling down barn; an old priest served it but no one seems to have been sufficiently interested in it to maintain it. Its only treasure was a painted crucifix (now preserved in Santa Chiara, Assisi). Francis knelt before this and meditated on the Passion of Christ, and the message came to him, 'Francis! Do you not see that my house is falling down? Repair it!' Here was something practical, an answer to the nagging question, 'What shall I do?' He did not see then any deeper meaning in the message. For him 'Repair' meant putting the building itself in repair. As a first step, he gave money to the priest for oil so that a lamp might be kept burning before the crucifix. More money would be needed for the actual repair work. Francis went home, and, in his father's absence, took some bales of cloth from the warehouse and rode with them to the market at Foligno. He sold the cloth and the horse and hastened back on foot to San Damiano and handed the money to the priest who, however, refused to accept such a large sum; he was a prudent man as he sensed there might be trouble with Pietro Bernadone; so Francis left the money on the window sill. All that the priest would agree to was that Francis should come and live with him. This alone must have troubled the priest as he would be well aware of Francis's reputation.

There are several aspects of this curious episode that call for consideration. Technically Francis had stolen his father's property; perhaps 'stolen' is too hard a word as the spoilt young man must have come to regard the family merchandise as being at his disposal; he had only to ask and his wishes were met. Whatever money he needed had been given to him. It is true that his father was away at the time, but money must have been available. Was it that he wished to earn the money he wanted to give away? His thoughts, it will be noted, were still on money as the means for putting things right. In the end, as we shall see, he came to abhor money, it may have seemed to him to have been one cause for his indifferent religious life. The episode reflects his mental and spiritual confusion.

When Pietro returned from his journey, he was angry at what had happened. Would he have been as angry if Francis had taken some cloth for some new clothes? For some time Pietro had been troubled at Francis's behaviour. As the eldest son he would inherit the business but he was frequently off on his own affairs and seemingly associating with the dregs of society. Now he had gone beyond reason and must be brought to heel. Pietro may seem at first sight to have been the heavy father and he certainly went to extremes — a characteristic his son shared with him. In one way the father had only himself to thank; the indulgence he allowed to Francis was unwise. When Pietro heard that his son was living at San Damiano, he sought the aid of some friends and set out to bring him home. Someone warned Francis and, rather than face his father, he concealed himself in a cave where he remained in hiding for some weeks. Only one friend, no doubt the unnamed companion of his earlier withdrawals, knew where he was and brought him food. Francis had flinched at this first threat, but by prayer and meditation he gained the courage to return openly to Assisi. People mocked his unkempt appearance and his bedraggled clothes; some declared he must be crazed in his wits. His father seized him, beat him, manacled him and imprisoned him in his house. Francis remained unshaken by his father's threats and the pleadings of his mother, but she, sensing something of her son's spiritual resolution, set him free as soon as Pietro left on a trading journey. On his return he was angry with her but was more determined than ever to prove himself the master. Once more he went down to San Damiano where Francis had again found refuge. He made no attempt to evade his father this time and went to meet him. After some harsh words and even blows, Pietro proposed a bargain whereby Francis would disinherit himself but at the same time return the money he had given to San Damiano. Francis was very willing to renounce all claims on the business but declared that he could not return money that now belonged to the Church. Pietro lodged a complaint with the civic authorities whose jurisdiction in a church matter Francis refused to recognise. His father then cited him before the bishop's court.

Bishop Guido of Assisi was intent on maintaining the rights of the Church — perhaps too intent at times — but he had an understanding heart. He must have known all about Francis who had become the talk and, as some would say, the scandal of the town; it is probable that the priest at San Damiano had consulted the bishop in what was a delicate situation, and it may be that Francis himself had earlier discussed his spiritual perplexities with him. Indeed, the bishop's handling of the problem suggests that he was prepared. The case was not a simple one; the complainant was among the leading merchants in what was a relatively small community; the son's strange conduct was contrary to all social conventions. To whatever extent the bishop may have been prepared, he must have been startled at what happened when father and son stood before him, yet he preserved his evenness of judgment. Bishop Guido pointed out to Francis that it was only right for him to return money that had been obtained in such an irregular manner. 'Have faith in the Lord, my son,' he said. 'Play the man and fear not, for He Himself will be your helper and give you whatever is necessary for the work of the Church.'

Francis then handed back the money and declared that he would return not only the money but the very clothes he owned to his father. He then stripped himself bare and in doing so revealed that he wore a hair shirt. Pietro took the money and the clothes; the onlookers, who so far had sided with him, murmured when they saw that he had not left his son anything to wear. The bishop took off his own cloak and put it around Francis, and from then onwards he gave this eccentric young man his support and sympathy.

This confrontation may seem to us somewhat theatrical, but men were like that in the twelfth century; they tended to go to extremes and to display their feelings dramatically, sometimes violently.

The episode marks a decisive stage in Francis's way of life.

He was then about twenty-four years old. The bishop had thrown his cloak over him not only literally but metaphorically. To Francis the approbation or at least the acquiescence of the Church was a primary need. As we shall see, he worked within the Church, never against it, and he always gave due respect to a priest even to one who was unworthy in his day-to-day life. The bishop's protection also quelled the general hostility of the Assisians; not that Francis was to escape ridicule and even persecution, but these were to be sporadic outbursts. He left the bishop's palace wearing a servant's tunic; he was now free to follow wherever the grace of God would lead him.

2.

The First Companions

FRANCIS, rejoicing in his freedom, set off up the valley of the Tescio to the mountains; it was a wild and unfrequented way and he rejoiced in the freshness of the countryside in spring; he was always responsive to the beauty of nature. As he went he sang the Provençal songs he enjoyed so much. Suddenly some robbers stopped him, stripped him of all but his shirt and flung him into a gulley in which some of the winter snow still lingered. He made his way to a near-by monastery (perhaps Santa Maria della Rocca near Valfabbrica) and asked for work in the kitchen in return for food and some old clothing. He was treated so brusquely that he left and walked on to Gubbio where an old friend provided him with a tunic, belt, wallet, sandals and staff. So garbed he returned to Assisi and San Damiano. There he set to work repairing the chapel.He would go into Assisi and beg for building stone, not, it is significant, for money. A few still mocked him but others gave him what he needed. The labour of carrying the stone and of building up the walls did not come easily to one who had never done any manual work and the results must have been botched for want of skill. The old priest noticed that Francis was eating too little so, quietly, out of his slender means, he provided more nourishing food. When Francis realised what was happening, he praised the priest's charity and thoughtfulness, but determined that he must himself find the necessary food. He took a dish and went from door to door in Assisi begging for left-overs and scraps. This fresh abasement was a real trial to him as it was to be to those who followed him. The sight of what was given him on this first occasion revolted him, but he conquered his nausea and ate the broken meats. Occasional meetings with his father were unavoidable in such begging rounds, but Pietro Bernadone cursed his son and passed on. We know no more of the family.

When the rough patching-up of San Damiano was finished, Francis turned his attention to another decayed chapel nearby, perhaps San Pietro della Spina, and having restored that, he went to a third, Santa Maria della Porziuncola — Saint Mary of the Little Portion, now Santa Maria degli Angeli. It was down on the plain two miles from Assisi. This secluded and ancient chapel was surrounded by woodlands and there Francis could pray and meditate in those surroundings that meant so much to him when the world seemed to press too closely on him. The chapel was also near the lazar-house where he continued to minister to the lepers. It is difficult for us to picture the Porziuncola as it was in those days; it is now enshrined in the great basilica of St Mary of the Angels; unhappily a number of well-meaning but surely misguided artists have embellished the exterior of the cradle of the Friars Minor; in spite of this, this tiny chapel can speak to us.

At length the chapel was sufficiently repaired for Mass to be said there occasionally. It was on the Feast of St Matthias, the 24th February, that Francis was to receive the divine intimation of the next stage of his spiritual enlightenment. The Gospel of the day was St Matthew 10:7-19. Verse 9 read, 'Do not provide gold or silver or copper to fill your purses, nor a wallet for the journey, no second coat, no spare shoes or staff.' Francis asked the priest to expound the reading. Here was the solution of the money problem — do without it! And the solution of how to dress. This message was meant for him. He gave away his tunic, his belt and wallet, his sandals and even his staff. He made himself a habit of the coarsest cloth and marked it with a cross; a rope replaced the belt and he went barefooted. So he came utterly to renounce the pride of his youth, he who had loved to dress in the finest cloth and to entertain his friends lavishly. It had been a long and agonising search but now at last the link with his earlier life was broken once for all. The records are not sufficiently precise for dating the stages of Francis' spiritual progress; this determinative hearing of the Gospel took place about 1208 — that is as near as we can go. Francis was then twenty-six years of age.

He took to heart another verse of that Gospel. 'Preach as you go, telling the Kingdom of Heaven is at hand.' So he went back to Assisi and greeted all with the words 'The Lord give you peace.' He preached first in the church of San Giorgio where some seventeen years later he was to be entombed. His message was simple and based on the Gospel call to repentance. In his scanty writings and in the traditions of his preaching there are few references to the Epistles or to the Old Testament; the Gospels, which he seems to have known by heart, gave him all he needed, and, so he believed, all the world needed.

His own joy in this new-found spiritual peace affected others as much as his preaching influenced them; this power of communicating his own inner happiness was one of the notable traits in his personality. Though he needed periods of solitude to search the mystery of Christ's Gospel, he also needed companionship so that he could share his experience with others. It is probable that some friends had occasionally helped him in his labours as a restorer of neglected chapels, and it may be that the unnamed friend of his early time of turmoil continued his companionship; he may have been the Peter that is mentioned (but not Peter Catanii, who came later). Others may have come out of curiosity to see this transformed Francis Bernadone and may have been won over to sympathise with him. Some, perhaps, 'who came to scoff, remained to pray'.

Bernard of Quintavalle, a prosperous merchant and magistrate of Assisi, was the first companion of repute. He had been impressed by the total change in Francis's life and by his refreshingly simple interpretation and application of the Gospel message. But was it a permanent change? Could this be but another passing caprice? Francis had not been noted for his stability in the past. Bernard and Francis must have known one another intimately for Francis agreed to lodge with Bernard when he stayed overnight in Assisi. They shared a bedroom. One night Bernard pretended to be asleep so that he could watch his companion. He saw that Francis, after a brief rest, got up and became absorbed in prayer until dawn. This was the final proof to Bernard of his friend's regeneration, and he declared his intention of following his example. What was God's will for them? Prayer would reveal this to them. So the next morning they went to the church of St Nicholas taking Peter with them. Francis prayed that God would show them his will from the pages of the Gospels. At the first opening he read,

> 'If thou hast a mind to be perfect, go home and sell all that belongs to thee; give it to the poor, and so the treasure that thou hast shall be in heaven; then come back and follow me.' (Matt. 19:21).

At the second opening were the words that had already gone to Francis's heart.

> 'Take nothing with you to use on your journey, staff or wallet or bread or money; you are not to have more than one coat apiece.' (Lk. 9:3)

And at the third opening,

> 'If any man has a mind to come my way, let him renounce self, and take up his cross, and follow me.' (Matt. 16:24).

'Here', said Francis, 'is our life and rule, and for all who join us. Let us fulfil it.'

Bernard at once arranged to sell all his goods and give the money to the poor. This sale was a sensation in Assisi; many, especially the better-off, must have shaken their heads at such quixotic behaviour and must have thought that Bernard had taken leave of his senses. The priest of St Nicholas was in the crowd. His name was Sylvester, and he had supplied Francis with some of the stone used at San Damiano; now he suggested that some of this money was due to him in payment. Francis gave him a handful of coins. Sylvester went home well satisfied, but the incident troubled him, and the time was to come when he would be one of the Fratres Minores.

Others came to Francis and asked to share his life. There was Leo, a priest, Giles, a farm worker, and Sabbatino, Morico of the lazar-house, John of Capella, and John the Long. The Porziuncola became their home and in the woods around it they made shacks such as the shepherds used as shelters.

What manner of man was Francis? There is no portrait that can be accepted as convincing. The earliest (at the Sacra Speco at Subiaco) was painted, it is thought, about two years after his death. It shows no very distinctive features and might well be labelled simply ' a friar.' The so-called portraits have in fact little in common.[1] There is, however, a carefully composed description of Francis by Thomas of Celano,[2] who wrote the first official biography within three years of Francis's death. He had joined the friars about four or five years after the first companions; his account is the only first-hand one we have. It reads;

'He was charming in his manners, of gentle disposition, easy in his talk; most apt in exhortation, most faithful in what he was put in trust with, far-seeing in counsel,

[1]The terra-cotta statue by Andrea della Robbia (d. 1525) in Santa Maria degli Angeli, is a lovely piece of work and has been frequently reproduced; it is too sentimentalised.
[2]The author of the *Dies irae*. A later Franciscan poet, Jacopone da Todi (d.1306) wrote the *Stabat mater*. Neither ascription is absolutely certain, but highly probable.

effectual in business, gracious in all things; calm in mind, sweet in temper, sober in spirit, uplifted in contemplation, assiduous in prayer, and fervent in all things. He was stedfast in purpose, firm in virtue, persevering in grace, and in all things the same.

He was swift to pardon and slow to be angry. He was of ready wit, and had an excellent memory, he was subtle in discussion, circumspect in choice, and simple in all things; stern to himself, tender to others, in all things discreet. He was a man most eloquent, of cheerful countenance, of kindly aspects, free from cowardice, and destitute of arrogance.

He was of middle height, inclining to shortness, his head was of moderate size and round; his face somewhat long and prominent, his forehead smooth and small; his eyes were black, of moderate size, and with a candid look; his hair was dark, his eyebrows straight; his nose symmetrical, thin and straight; his ears upright, but small; his temples smooth. His words were kindly but fiery and penetrating; his voice was powerful, sweet-toned, clear and sonorous. His teeth were set close together, white, and even, his lips thin and fine, his beard black and rather scanty, his neck slender; his shoulders straight, his arms short, his hands attenuated, with long fingers and nails; his legs slight, his feet small, his skin fine, and his flesh very spare. His clothing was rough, his sleep very brief, his hand most bountiful. And, for that he was most humble, he showed all meekness to all men, adapting himself in profitable fashion to the behaviour of all' (I, para. 83, Thomas of Celano).

3.

Papal Acquiescence

THIS small group of brethren had now to discover the way of life they should follow. Francis did not make a time-table nor frame a set of regulations. There was a preliminary or experimental period. He was content to wait while the Holy Spirit shaped their lives for them. They rose before dawn after a few hours of sleep; each prayed and meditated in silence, then they separated for whatever seemed the best way of using their time. Work among the lepers continued. The problem of food had to be faced. One solution was to work in the fields or farms and receive their pay in kind, for Francis was determined that they must not touch money. So they were given vegetables or fruit or, on at least one occasion, a sack of walnuts. This was seasonal work, so at other times they had to go begging round the farms or in Assisi, but it was proving less easy to get alms in the town; the citizens began to grumble at supporting these men who chose to be penniless. The murmuring reached the ears of Bisho Guido who sent for Francis. The bishop pointed out that it was not prudent to have no means of support and to rely on charity; monks had their monasteries and supported themselves, but Francis and his companions had no home and no resources. Francis then stated a principle from which he never diverged though it was to lead to much trouble in the future. 'My lord, ' he said, 'if we own property we shall have to defend it and be led into squabbles and perhaps lawsuits. As this will prevent us from loving God and our neighbour with our whole hearts as, by his grace, we intend to do, we prefer to possess nothing.' The bishop was not convinced; perhaps he thought that experience would soon prove that total poverty was impracticable; nonetheless he gave Francis his blessing.

In the autumn of 1209 Francis decided that the time had come for them to go out to the people. He said, ' God has called us not so much for our own salvation as for that of others. Let us then go about urging people by our words and our example to do penance and obey God's commandments. Do not worry because you feel weak and foolish, but preach repentance in simple words trusting in the Lord that through his Spirit he will tell you what to say.' He warned them that they must expect opposition and even persecution. 'In your hearts, bear all things patiently.'

He himself with an unnamed companion set off up the valley of Rieti, Francis singing in praise of God. As he expected, they were roughly treated by some and were refused shelter so they had at times to spend the nights sheltering in church porches; others, however, listened to them and respected their mission. They climbed up the stony track to the village of Poggio-Bustone on a spur of the Apennines. They greeted the people with the words, 'Good morning, good people.' This is now recorded by an inscription:

BUONO GIORNO, BUONA GENTE
Saluto rivolto da San Francesco
entrando a Poggio Bustone
nel 1209

Here he felt impelled to leave his companion for a period of solitude; he went above the town and found a grotto where he could pray and meditate, repeating time and again the words 'God be merciful to me, a sinner.' Then a great joy seized him; he was assured of forgiveness and he had a vision of 'a great multitude of men coming to us, and desiring to live with us in the habit of holy life and under the rule of blessed religion.'

We can see the life of St Francis as a series of spiritual crises.

He was never content to rest at any one stage with the assurance at which he had now arrived. He must ever press onwards seeking to sound the depths of the meaning of Our Lord's life, teaching and Passion. He was early convinced of a few simple truths — the call to repentance and a change of life in humility and obedience, and, for him and his companions, poverty. Francis believed that as the Gospel message was given to ordinary folk as they crowded round Jesus, so they would respond to the same message if it was put to them in plain language without any of the subtle refinements of the theologians. He himself was ignorant of the writings of the Fathers, and, indeed, he feared that the simplicity of the Gospel message could be obscured by the nice distinctions of the learned, a point of view that was to create difficulties in later years.

In the spring of 1210 the companions reassembled at the Porziuncola. A knight of Rieti, Angelo Tancredi, had come with Francis and the numbers of followers increased to eleven. Francis, who was determined to work under the authority of the Church, now decided they should go to Rome and seek the blessing of the Pope. So they set off on the fifty mile journey, barefooted and clothed in their tunics of natural coloured coarse cloth, though there was probably no uniform design at this period. Francis also decided that they must have a leader, a position he refused to take; so they chose Bernard, the first who joined him. Actually we hear nothing more of this leadership in the early days; as we shall see, at Rome it was Francis who was the spokesman; perhaps Bernard organised the foraging and shelter. It was a cheerful journey for they sang and joked on the way; they spoke their simple message to any who would listen to them and they frequently turned aside for periods of quiet prayer.

The Pope was Innocent III who had been elected in 1198. Of him it has been written, 'Few have equalled him in the capacity to administer, judge, negotiate, and decide in affairs political and ecclesiastical involving all Europe.'

When the companions reached Rome, Francis at once went to the Lateran to speak to the Pope. By such a direct approach, Francis was breaking curial protocol and he was rebuffed. It so chanced that later he met his own bishop who was in Rome on diocesan affairs. Bishop Guido was at first annoyed that Francis had not sought his advice before setting out, but no one could be angry with Francis for long, and the bishop was genuinely sympathetic even if a bit sceptical. He knew that little could be done without the help of one of the cardinals, so he took Francis to see Cardinal John of St Paul, Bishop of Sabina. At first the Cardinal urged Francis to merge his little band in one of the existing orders, but after several conversations Cardinal John sensed that here was a new approach to the faith that might rejuvenate the Church. He himself was a man of devout life and worked to remove some of the abuses of the times. So he took Francis to see the Pope and the attendant cardinals. They listened to Francis's explanation of the kind of life he and his companions wished to follow. At once it was objected that the vow of utter poverty was impracticable. The Pope would not give an immediate decision; he dismissed Francis saying, 'Pray, my son, to Christ, that through you his will may be revealed; when we know what it is, we shall more safely comply with your pious wishes.'

Francis and his companions took themselves to prayer; this strengthened their resolution. When Francis next came before the Pope he put before him this parable.

'A poor but beautiful woman lived in the wilderness. A king, passing by, was so impressed by her beauty that he stooped to marry her; they had several sons who continued to live with their mother far from the court in ignorance of their father's high position. When they had grown to be men, she said to them, "Have no fear, the king

is your father. Go to him and he will provide for you."
When they came to court the king was struck by their
handsome appearance. "Who are you?" he asked. "We
are the sons of the poor woman who lives in the
wilderness." The king was glad. "If I feed strangers at my
table," he said, "shall I not more readily feed you, my own
sons?" (*Three Companions*, para. 50)

Francis added, 'That great king is God, and I am the poor
woman by whom he longs to have true sons.' The Pope and
the cardinals were at first rather shocked at this analogy, but
the Pope recalled a recent dream that troubled him. He had
seen the great Lateran basilica about to fall down, but it was
supported on the shoulders of a poorly clothed religious. We
can see a parallel here with the message Francis had received
at San Damiano. 'Do you not see my house is falling down?'
So the Pope gave his verbal consent to the Rule drawn up by
Francis. The brethren were to preach repentance to the
people but were not to expound dogma. 'When your numbers
have increased, come to me again, and you shall have greater
powers.' Francis pledged his obedience to the Pope and the
companions, at the Pope's command, pledged their
obedience to Francis, and to his successors. These neophytes
were then given the first tonsure; thus they became clerics (not
priests) and were put under the protection of the Church. It
was probably then that Francis was ordained deacon.

No copy of this original Rule has survived; it was the basis
for the extended Rule of 1221', and a careful examination of
this makes it possible, with reasonable accuracy, to see what
Francis put before the Pope in 1210. It should be noted that
this primitive Rule was unlike those of existing Orders; thus
the Benedictine Rule laid down details for liturgical
observances and for administration under a hierarchy of
officers. Francis was intent on getting the spirit right and left
problems of organisation to be dealt with as they arose. He was

not a legislator like St Benedict, but was satisfied if his followers shared what he was convinced were the fundamental but simple principles of the spiritual life that had brought him assurance during his long struggle to gain enlightenment and to free himself from the trammels of the world.

Only a brief summary is possible here.

1. The brothers live in obedience, in chastity, and without property.

2. A new brother must sell all he has and give to the poor.

3. All should be dressed in the poorest clothes.

4. No brother may have any power over anyone, least of all over one of his fellows.

5. Those who have skill shall work; no money is to be accepted; if necessary, like other brothers, they should beg alms.

6. Brothers do not speak ill of others, nor do they dispute among themselves.

7. When they go on journeys to preach, they may not take with them either purse or money, not even a staff. They must give away even their clothes if asked.

8. All clerics and priests and religious must be held in respect.

The final admonition with its echoes from the Gospels must be given in full (as far as this can be determined) as it goes to the heart of the message of St Francis.

'This and similar exhortation and praise, all my brothers may announce with the blessing of God whenever it shall please them and wherever they may be. "Fear and honour, praise and bless, give thanks unto and adore the Lord God Almighty in Trinity and Unity, Father, Son and Holy Spirit, Creator of all. Do penance; bring forth fruits worthy of penance, and know that you will all soon die. Give and it shall be given unto you. Forgive and you shall be forgiven. And if you will not forgive men their sins neither will the Lord forgive you your sins. Blessed are they who shall die in penance for they shall be in the kingdom of heaven. Woe to those who shall not die in penance, because they shall be the children of the devil, whose works they do, and they shall go into everlasting fire. Beware, and abstain from all evil and persevere unto the end in good."' (*Cuthbert*, p.106)

It may have been this last injuction that led the Pope to hope that this new approach to the reawakening of the faith among the people must be given its opportunity.

4.

The Return to the Porziuncola

THE companions set off from Rome in a joyful mood; the Pope had approved their apostolate and now they had his authority to preach to the people. They followed the Tiber on their return journey, and near Orte, about forty miles on their way, they found a pleasant place, well away from men, where they could talk over their future plans; indeed it was so pleasant there that they were tempted to linger, but after a fortnight of what may be called a retreat in preparation for their ministry, they continued their journey. It is not known why they did not at once go to the Porziuncola; the disturbed state of the country with the Emperor Otho ravaging Umbria may have kept them away from that part. Instead they chose a disused hut near Rivo-Torto in the plain below Assisi; the shelter was so cramped that Francis marked with chalk the narrow space each used. The site of this hut has not been determined with certainty. The claims of the present church at Rivo-Torto are disputed; it seems more likely that their hut or shed was near the San Rufino d'Arce and Santa Maria Maddalena; from there they could resume their care of the lepers.

The term 'companions' has been used so far; when did they become Fratres Minores? Perhaps this was settled on their way from Rome; now that the Pope recognised them, they needed a label. Francis decided on 'Fratres Minores' — the Lesser Brothers — thus emphasising that humility was a virtue they should cultivate and that they must not take on the duties of the higher clergy.

Their numbers increased while they were at Rivo-Torto, and it was then that some of the best-known Franciscans (a term Francis would not have liked) joined the brotherhood. Their exact order of joining is not known, but among them were Rufino, of a noble family, Massio, a big, handsome man, Illuminato from Arce and his friend Augustin, and Sylvester, the priest who had demanded payment when Bernard's goods were sold. Two of these are commemorated in Dante's *Paradiso* (xii, 130),

> *'Here, of the earliest of the barefoot poor,*
> *Illuminato and Augustin, made dear*
> *to God.'*

The coming of two priests was momentous; it not only removed any suggestion that the new brotherhood was opposed to the priesthood, but it meant that Mass was now said regularly and the friars could have the sacrament of penance at any time. Brother Leo was confessor to Francis, who did not himself become a priest. Leo seems to have been the scribe or secretary.

Not all who sought admission persevered and some did not understand the underlying purpose of the brotherhood. One such came to Rivo-Torto; he seldom prayed, nor did he work or go begging. We should call him a lay-about. At length Francis said to him 'Go your way, Brother Fly, since you are content to enjoy the work of others, but are a lazy and barren drone and content to profit from the work of the good bees.'

Francis and the brethren went preaching in Assisi and in the neighbouring villages and hamlets. He himself preached in San Giorgio and was later invited to give the Sunday sermon for several weeks in the cathedral. In spite of his insignificant appearance, Francis was a compelling preacher; there was no attempt at rhetoric, or an assumption of learning. His message was the simple Gospel of repentance. One later observer wrote, 'He spoke with such skill and eloquence that many of the best scholars there were filled with admiration at the words of so simple a man. Yet he had not the manner of a preacher, his ways being rather those of conversation.' It is significant that his sermons often had an immediate practical outcome. Thus he would urge his hearers to clean the church and put all in decent order, and he himself would be the first to take the broom. His influence went beyond such useful applications; he was able to bring together rival factions in Assisi and later in Perugia and persuade them to work together for the benefit of the town.

Two incidents of the life at Rivo-Torto serve to show how the brothers were still seeking to discover how they should live, and to reveal a trait in Francis's character that is sometimes overlooked — his commonsense. One night a friar cried out, 'I am dying!' The others woke and were alarmed. Francis asked him what was the reason for his cry. 'I die of hunger,' the friar replied. At once Francis ordered all the food they had to be collected and then with the afflicted man and the others, they all sat down to a meal. The fact was that some of them tended to go too far in asceticism. So Francis said to them, 'I bid each of you to consider his bodily needs and to take what food is necessary; some need more than others.' Some were imposing the most severe inflictions on themselves — extreme abstinence, long vigils, iron belts and hair shirts. Francis corrected these excesses, for an enfeebled friar could not endure the unavoidable privations of missionary journeys.

The second incident also concerned food. Francis noticed that one of the friars was weakening in health and was languid. He said to himself, 'If this brother would eat some ripe grapes early in the morning, I believe it would do him good.' So he got up early one day and took the friar to the neighbouring vineyard and ate some of the grapes himself in case his companion should be shy of eating alone. In both incidents we can see how Francis was anxious to avoid lowering the self-respect of a friar; if all had a meal together, the one who occasioned the meal would not feel singular; if he himself ate the grapes first, the other would not mind following his example.

Francis decided they must leave Rivo-Torto partly because their numbers were outgrowing the shelter, and also because a herdsman claimed its use. Where could they go? They needed a church where their priests could say Mass and where prayer and meditation would be fostered. He went to Bishop Guido, but the bishop had no church that was not in use. So Francis climbed up to the Benedictine monastery on Mount Subasio to whom the Porziuncola belonged; perhaps the abbot would let the friars use it as it was so small and neglected. The abbot gladly gave Francis permission, and added, 'If the Lord increases your numbers, then let the church of the Blessed Mary of the Porziuncola be your chief dwelling.' As a nominal rent the friars gave a basket of fish every year to the monks and they, in return, gave the friars a flask of oil. It may have been at that time that the abbot also gave permission for the use of San Damiano which belonged to the Benedictines. So the Fratres Minores went back to the Porziuncola and, as the abbot hoped, it became their rallying centre. This gift was made in 1211; a few years later the monks also added the Carceri, caverns either natural or artificial in the rocky side of a deep mountain gorge in the foothills of Monte Subasio and about a half-hour's climb from Assisi. A cluster of cells and chapels has grown up in this wild place, 'seeming as if,' it has been written, 'they hung from the bare rocks with nothing to prevent them falling straight into the depths of the ravine.' Here there was a hermitage or retreat where the brothers could retire secure from interruption and there renew their spiritual fervour. As we shall see, other such lonely and untamed places were to be found in later years. Thus Francis could meet two needs; he wanted such a centre as the Porziuncola where the friars could gather and for a while live together, but he wanted also secluded grottoes where it was possible to pray and meditate in silence amid the uncultivated beauties of nature.

The Porziuncola, or Santa Maria della Porziuncola, to give the full name, had a special place in the affections of Francis and in the story of the Fratres Minores. A few permanent cells of planks or stones were made though brushwood shelters were put up when there was a gathering of friars. One of the cells had been intended for Francis himself, but he rejected this notion; it savoured of property.

'On a day when he went out of that cell, a certain friar went to see it, and afterward came to the place where blessed Francis was. And when the blessed Father saw him, he said to him, "Whence do you come, brother?" And he said, "I come from your cell." And blessed Francis said, "For that you call it mine, another shall stay there henceforth, and not I." ' (*Speculum Perfectionis,* ix)

He himself said in later years when a Minister General had been appointed to manage the affairs of the Order.

'I would that this place should always be immediately under the power of the Minister General and servant, for the reason that he should have greater care and solicitude in providing there a good and holy family. Let clerks be chosen among the better and more holy and more fitting friars, those of the whole Order who can best say the Office, that not only lay folk but also the other friars may willingly and with great devotion see and hear them. But of the lay brothers, let holy men and discreet and humble and decent be chosen, who may serve them. I will also that no woman and no friar enter that place except the Minister General and the friars who serve them. And they shall not speak with any person, except with the friars who serve them and with the Minister who shall visit them. I will, likewise, that the lay brothers themselves who serve them, be bound never to say to them idle words of this world's news, or anything not useful to their souls. And on account of this, I especially will that no one shall enter into the dwelling, that they the better preserve its purity and sanctity, and that in that place nothing be said or done uselessly, but the whole place itself be preserved pure and holy in hymns and the praises of the Lord. And when any of those friars shall have passed away to the Lord, I will that in his place another holy friar, wherever he may be, be sent thither by the Minister General. For if the other friars shall have fallen off somewhat from purity and honesty, I will that this place be blessed, and that it remain ever a mirror and a good example of the whole Order, and like a candlestick before the throne of God and the blessed Virgin, always burning and shining. On account of which the Lord will have mercy on the defects and faults of all friars, and always preserve and protect this order and this His tender plant.' (*Speculum Perfectionis,* ch. VII)

After the death of Francis an unknown friar wrote a panegyric of the Porziuncola; the church had become known as Santa Maria degli Angeli, but there is no record of when or why the change was made; perhaps both names were used indifferently:

Holy of holies, truly is this place of places,
Worthily held worthy of great honours.
Happy its surname, more happy is its name.
And now its third name arises, omen of the gifts
The Angelic presence here casts abroad the light.
Here watches oft by night sounding hymns with the voice.
Afterward all fell in ruin. Francis raised it up again,
Out of the three it was one which the Father himself repaired.
This the Father chose when with sackcloth he clothed its members.
Here he broke the body and forced it to obey the mind.
Here by the fire of his love, he kindled our wills,
Here within the temple was begotten the Order, the minors.

While the Father's example a crowd of men doth follow.
Clara, the spouse of God was here the first time shorn,
Cast off the pomps of the world and followed Christ.
Here the renowned birth of brothers at once and of sisters.
The holy mother here by whom she brought back Christ to the
world.
Here was made narrow the broad road of the old world,
And virtue made wider for the chosen race.
Here grew the Rule; Holy Poverty reborn,
Pride smitten down, the cross called back among us.
Thus where was troubled Francis, and sore wearied,
here was he rested; his death was here renewed.
Here was he shown the truth whereof he doubted,
Nay, here was granted whatever that Father desired.
(Speculum Perfectionis, LXXXIV)

Settlement at the Porziuncola brought a fresh flow of
postulants. Among them were a hermit from Perugia, a rich
man from Cortona, a nobleman from Arezzo, and a doctor of
law and his son from Florence. Three call for particular
mention. Agnellus of Pisa led the mission to England in 1224,
and from the same city came Albert, a future Minister-
General of the Order. Then there was Elias of Assisi, a
mattress-maker and teacher of boys, whose later debatable
policies do not, fortunately, come within the scope of these
pages.

The first group of companions had been mostly Assisians;
now they were beginning to come from farther afield. It will
also be noted that they were of many sections of society — rich
and poor, learned and illiterate, noblemen and labourers.
Francis studied each of them with a shrewd appraisal. We
have seen him dismiss Brother Fly and no doubt others found
that they were unable to live the full life of a friar. In later
years Francis was asked to describe the perfect friar. He
replied with a series of thumbnail sketches of some of his early

companions. This passage is given in chapter 85 of the *Speculum Perfectionis.*

'He used to say that he would be a good Friar Minor who should have the life and conditions of these holy friars, to wit: the faith of Brother Bernard, which he had most perfectly, with the love of poverty: the simplicity and poverty of Brother Leo, who was truly of the holiest purity: the courtesy of Brother Angelo, who was the first noble who came into the Order, and who was adorned with all courtesy and benignity: the gracious and natural sense, with the fair and devout eloquence of Brother Masseo: the mind raised to contemplation which Brother Giles had in highest perfection: the virtuous and continual labour of holy Ruffino, who without intermission prayed always, for even when sleeping or doing anything, his mind was always with the Lord: the patience of Brother Juniper, who arrived at the perfect state of patience, because of the perfect truth of his own vileness which he had before his eyes: and the desire in the highest degree of imitating Christ through the bodily and spiritual strength of the cross, of Brother John of the Lauds, who in his time was strong of body of all men: the charity of Brother Roger, whose whole life and conversation was in the fervour of charity: and the solicitude of Brother Lucido, who was of the greatest solicitude, and was unwilling to stay in one place for a month, but when it pleased him to stay in any one place, immediately he went away from there, and said: "We have no dwelling-place here but in Heaven."'

When the friars gathered at the Porziuncola in 1217, there were some five thousand of them, many coming from foreign countries. Can we account for this phenomenal spread of the Friars Minor? For some years there had been mounting discontent with the Church. There were many devout priests who were wholly devoted to their calling; among the upper ranks of the hierarchy there were earnest bishops such as Bishop Guido of Assisi, and dedicated cardinals such as Cardinal John of St Paul. But there was the other side of the coin. There were priests who lived immoral or dissipated lives; there were those intent on place-and-power rather than on holiness. There were bishops and cardinals who lived in luxury and amassed wealth. When men appealed to Rome or even to their own bishop, they had to bribe their way from official to official. Where in this sordid ecclesiastical world was the spirit of Christ? So devout laymen turned their thoughts to the Gospels and the picture of the early Church set out in The Acts of the Apostles; they wanted to go back to the simple teaching of Jesus and to be rid of the accretions that were threatening to stifle the Church. Such men got together and formulated rules for plain living with charity as the guiding principle. Thus Peter of Waldo about 1170, ten years before the birth of Francis, founded the Poor Men of Lyons (known later as Waldensians); he gave away his wealth and preached privately and in the streets. His evangelism was based on a translation into French made at his request of the New Testament. In later years the Waldensians fell foul of the Church and were persecuted. Another group, about the same time, the Humiliati in Milanese territory, were also trying to live in keeping with the Gospels. As they submitted to the Holy See, the Pope, Innocent III allowed them to preach among themselves provided they kept to moral teaching and did not discuss doctrine. The Waldensians and the Humiliati lived in the world, marrying and carrying on their trades and crafts. We cannot here follow the later histories of these and similar lay groups; some lapsed into heresy.

How far Francis was aware of the contemporary Poor Men of Lyons and of the Humiliati is not known. His father may have come into contact with them, or heard of them, in his trading journeys and perhaps spoke of them on his return home. There is, however, no hint that Francis was influencd by anyone. His was a personal search within the Church and it led him to an irresistible urge to share his spiritual experiences with others, and the world was waiting for him.

These movements were expressions of a recurrent theme in the history of the Church — 'back to the Early Church', and 'back to the Gospels.' The Fratres Minores were another example of this periodic longing for a return to a simpler form of religion away from the elaborate ecclesiastical institution. This, however does not account for their phenomenal growth within a matter of a very few years. They might easily have gradually declined from their first fervour or even fallen into heresy as other movements had done. They came just at a time when a changing social environment needed them. The main factor was urbanization. Population was rapidly increasing. Trade and commerce were expanding. Pietro Bernadone was just one of a vast number of of merchants who found their markets outside Italy. Wealth became concentrated in the towns, and country folk, as their numbers increased, who could no longer find a living on the land, flocked to the centres of prosperity; many too were lured by the prospects of earning more money. This meant not only the physical expansion of the towns but the growth of poverty alongside flaunted wealth. It was a situation the churches failed to meet. The monasteries were mostly in the country; they had been able to care for the poor who came for help. Such relief was rarely available in the towns where private charitable groups as well as individuals did the best they could. The friars came at the right moment. They themselves were poor and they brought the comforts of religion to the destitute and inspired the well-to-do to recognise a religious duty in succouring the needy and the sick. Something will be said later of the Third Order, here it must suffice to say that it was the preaching of the friars and their example that brought layfolk to wish to share in their ideals and labours.

An interesting parallel can be drawn with the situation in England when, in the eighteenth century, the Industrial Revolution was beginning to affect society; population was on the increase and the new work available in towns drew the people from the countryside into conditions of overcrowding and disease for which the state had made no provision. The Methodist movement met a need that the Established Church failed to satisfy or, often, even to acknowledge. There was, however one great difference between Wesley's work and the movement begun by Francis. The Methodists, against Wesley's wish, were, after his death, forced out of the Anglican Church and so became a new sect. By contrast, Pope Innocent III and his successors, sensed that the Fratres Minors, as loyal sons, could bring new life into the Church; so they were absorbed and encouraged and not rejected.

5.

Let Us Set Out In God's Name

THE acceptance of poverty and humility as the way of life for the Friars Minor, if regarded by itself, must seem a grim vocation; it was certainly a severe test of sincerity and of spiritual fervour. This is only one expression of the Franciscan spirit. The gaiety of his unregenerate youth never deserted Francis; it was transformed into the joy of religious conviction; it was shown in his intense love for mankind and for all living creatures and for the woods, the fields and the mountains. There are many stories of him that show how this joy was always breaking out. One example must suffice.

'For the most sweet melody of spirit boiling up within him frequently broke out in French speech and the veins of murmuring which he heard secretly with his ears, broke forth into French-like rejoicing. And sometimes he picked up a branch from the earth, and laying it on his left arm, he drew in his right hand another stick like a bow over it, as if on a viol or other instrument, and making fitting gestures, sang with it in French unto the Lord Jesus Christ.' (*Speculum Perfectionis*, XCIII)

This joy he passed on to his companions and so to others, telling them that their renewed or new-found faith should make them cheerful and not miserable: he called them 'God's gleemen'.

Francis knew the effect of visual representation. It was an age when most people were illiterate; indeed probably many of the friars of the first generation were unable to read or write. The painted pictures on the church walls, the storied windows, the liturgical ceremonies and processions and the

43

miracle plays were all means for instructing the people. This appeal of arresting even dramatic action was used by Francis not only in the training and education of his companions, but of the people as well. One incident from many will illustrate his dramatic method which at times startled and even shocked. He never spared himself in his struggle for spiritual perfection; he believed that his companions should be equally relentless on themselves. The measure of his influence is shown by how few failed in the formative period of the Order. This constant striving to remove weaknesses did not mean that the friars were being moulded into one form. The passage quoted in which Francis particularised some of his companions is evidence that he treasured individual excellencies in their variety. We know some of them by their distinctive personalities; such were the three companions who recorded their recollections — Leo, Angelo and Rufino; to these we can add Giles and Juniper as well as others.

An incident in the life of Brother Ruffino illustrates the points just made. He came of one of the leading families of Assisi; he was 'so absorbed in God, that he became as it were insensible and dumb, spake but seldom, and had neither the gift of preaching, nor boldness nor eloquence therein'. Francis ordered Ruffino 'by holy obedience' to go to Assisi wearing only his breeches and preach in one of the churches. The friar was mocked as he made his way through the streets; the people laughed at him and said among themselves, 'These fellows have become fools and are out of their wits.' Meanwhile Francis regretted the harshness of the task he had imposed on Ruffino, so he straightway decided that he himself must do what he had ordered the friar to do. He took off his habit and set off for Assisi; Brother Leo went with him carrying both habits. Francis too was jeered at, but he joined Ruffino in the pulpit.

'Then Francis went up into the pulpit, and began to

preach so marvellously of the contempt of the world, of
holy penitence, of voluntary poverty, and of the desire of
the kingdom of heaven, and of the nakedness and shame of
the passion of our Lord Jesus Christ, that all they that
heard the preaching, men and women in great multitude,
began to weep most bitterly with devout and contrite
hearts. And the people being thus edified and comforted
by this act of Francis and Brother Ruffino, Francis re-clad
Ruffino and himself; and so re-clad, they returned to the
Porziuncola, praising and glorifying God that had given
them the grace to overcome themselves, and to edify the
little sheep of Christ by good example, and to show how
greatly the world is to be despised.' (*Fioretti*, XXX)

This incident is typical. Francis exacted from Ruffino an
embarrassing proof of his humility and obedience; it was an
act that caught the attention of the people, even though at
first they jeered; so they crowded into the church to see the
fun. Then Francis, fearing that he had asked too much of a
brother, imposed the same action on himself. The ridicule of
the people led to an increase in their religious understanding.

Among the Assisians who were inspired by the preaching of
Francis and the friars was the eldest daughter of one of the
wealthy and influential families of the town; the men were
noted for their military prowess. Her name was Clare; she was
born in 1194 and was thus twelve years younger than Francis.
It is not known when she sought her first interview with him.
She desired above all to dedicate herself to the service of God,
not by entering one of the established Orders, but in some way
in keeping with the ideals of the Friars Minor. This presented
a peculiar problem to Francis; it had not been difficult in a
practical way for him to break away from his family; a man
could go his own way; but how could this girl be helped? They
must have worked out a plan of action. The situation was
delicate, for it might very easily have brought scandal on the

friars. On Palm Sunday, the 18th March 1212, Clare, dressed as befitted her rank, went to the cathedral to High Mass and the distribution of palms, but when the people processed up to the altar to receive the palms, she felt unable to move. Bishop Guido came down from the altar and gave her the palm. This unusual action suggests that the bishop may have had some inkling of the step Clare was about to take.

A sympathetic aunt was her confidante, and that night they left home by a side door and walked down to the Porziuncola where Francis and the friars, with torches, were waiting. Clare knelt at the altar and there vowed herself to God. Francis cut off her hair as a sign of her withdrawal from the world. It was like the first tonsure of a cleric. This could not be a canonical reception as Francis was only a deacon, and, of course there was no Order into which Clare could be received. The friars then took her to the nearby Benedictine convent of St Paul (even the site is unknown); the nuns must have had warning of what was to happen; one can see the whole business as a kind of holy conspiracy involving quite a number of people. Presumably the return of the aunt, no doubt escorted by a friar, gave the alarm and the next day some of Clare's kinsmen arrived at the convent to demand her return. She clung to the altar and removed her veil to reveal her shorn head. This must have shocked them and they saw that further argument was useless.

After a few days Clare went to the convent of Sant' Angelo di Panso on the slope of Monte Subasio outside Assisi. Here she was joined by her younger sister Agnes who had also resolved to leave the world. This second flight enraged her father, her brother and an uncle. With some retainers they went to the convent and laid rough hands on Agnes; she resisted with all her strength, and when Clare intervened, the men withdrew.

Meanwhile Francis and the friars were busy preparing San Damiano as a home for the two sisters and for those who might join them. The chapel belonged to the Benedictines of Monte Subasio and they had given permission for its use. The old priest whom Francis had helped in the early days of his new life, had presumably died, so his house was empty. The two sisters were soon joined by several other ladies of Assisi. In later years, Clare's mother, when widowed, entered San Damiano with her youngest daughter Beatrice. It was an enclosed convent, for, at that period, and for long after, there was no thought of nuns going about on errands of charity. Two or three lay sisters made the necessary contacts with the outside world. The friars begged for them and their priests ministered to them. In the early days Francis kept in touch with Clare and directed her own devotions and those of the little community. They became known as the 'Poor Ladies of San Damiano'. They had no history during the lifetime of St Francis; they were sequestered from the world. Later we hear of lay-brothers who made the outside contacts; probably the earlier lay-sisters had become absorbed in the community. The friars took it in turns to provide confessors and to say Mass. Francis himself could rarely have been there as he was constantly on the move. Those who visit the convent nowadays are deeply moved at the stark simplicity of the rough tables and benches; the sisters lived in mortifying poverty. For forty years until her death Clare remained at San Damiano. In 1217 her sister Agnes went as abbess to a convent near Florence but she returned in time to be at Clare's death-bed in 1253; she herself died shortly afterwards. Both have been canonized.

The friars went in pairs or threes when on their preaching missions. Brother Masseo seems to have been the frequent companion of Brother Francis. They tramped up and down central Italy and, on one occasion, went to Rome. Many must have smiled to see them together for they made a contrast. Masseo was tall and handsome, a fine looking man; Francis was short and, as one contemporary noted, 'his person was unprepossessing, and his face far from handsome.' No doubt they themselves got some amusement out of this dissimilarity and Francis would at times tease his companion. On one occasion they came to crossroads, one leading to Arezzo, the second to Sienna and the third to Florence. 'Which way now, Father?' asked Masseo. 'By that which the Lord wills,' replied Francis. 'But how can we know the will of God?' 'By a sign I will show you. Under obedience I order you to stand at the crossroads and turn round and round as little children do, and not stop until I tell you.' Masseo turned and turned until he went dizzy. Francis, with his eyes shut, at last said, 'Stop, and don't move. Now in which direction are you facing?' 'Towards Sienna.' So they went to Sienna and, such was Francis' influence, he was able to reconcile two rival factions there.

Their visit to Cortona brought a recruit. Francis preached to the people, for whenever word went round that he had come, all flocked to hear him. Among them was a wealthy youth named Guy who was noted for his charity to the poor. He invited the two friars to lodge with him and he himself brought water to wash off the dust from their feet and then he served them. Afterwards he begged Francis to let him become a friar. After their conversation Francis said to his companion, 'This noble youth who is so loving and courteous towards his neighbours and the poor, would do well for our company, for courtesy is one of the attributes of God, who in his courtesy, gives his rain to the just and unjust, and courtesy is the sister of charity by which hatred is extinguished and love is cherished. I have seen so much divine virtue in this man, I would gladly have him as a companion.'

So Guy gave away his possessions, and received the habit of a friar. He had evidently thought long about taking this step for he had already marked some caves in a ravine near Cortona as an ideal place for a life of prayer. There he lived for many years and became a priest. From time to time he would climb up to Cortona and preach to the people. Other friars came to stay with him when they needed to get away from the bustle of life on the road and in the towns. The Celle (cells) di Cortona are now a friary still revealing much of the primitive character of a Franciscan hermitage.

It may have been about this time, though chronology is uncertain, that Francis kept a Lenten fast of forty days, alone on Isola Maggiore in Lake Trasimene.

Francis had so far limited his evangelisation to central Italy. It may have been the Spanish victory of Las Navas di Tolosa in July 1212 that turned his thoughts to the conversion of the infidels. That battle spelt the end of the Moorish domination of the Peninsular. The Pope hoped that a new Crusade could now be launched against the Moslems in the East. The Fourth Crusade, which has been called the Crusade against Christians, had ended in the shameful ravaging of Constantinople in 1204 which had made absolute the division between the Western and Eastern Churches. The expulsion of the Moors from Spain seemed to promise well for a renewed offensive against Islam. Francis, however, did not wait for any organised Crusade; he decided to go to Syria. When he had made up his mind to go anywhere, he just went; there were no detailed preparations. All he did on this occasion was to appoint Peter Catanii to act for him during his absence. Then, in the autumn of 1212, he set out with a companion, probably Masseo, to walk to Ancona where they took ship, but a storm drove them on to the coast of Dalmatia from where there was no prospect of a passage to Syria; it was even difficult to get back to Italy as they had no money. Francis enlisted the help of some sailors who smuggled the two friars on board so they returned as stowaways. It was clear to him that he was not, at that time, to be permitted to reach the Moslems in the East.

On his return Francis preached in the Marches of Ancona and in Umbria, and eventually reached San Leo in the

Romagna about fifty miles north-west of Assisi, on a spur of the Apennines. When he and his companion arrived there they found that the little fortress town was celebrating the knighting of its lord with a tourney and all kinds of rejoicing. Francis preached to the people but had no wish to spoil their festivity; this kind of celebration must have recalled the days when he too hoped to win his knighthood. Among the guests was Orlando, lord of Chiusi; he told Francis that he wished to consult with him on his spiritual state. Francis was very willing but 'you must now do honour to your friends and dine with them; afterwards we will talk together.' At the end of their conversation Orlando said that he had a mountain named La Verna about twenty miles east of Florence, and near the source of the Tiber, which he would like to give to the friars; it was a wild and desolate part and would be ideal for a retreat. Francis gladly accepted the gift; the deed gives the date, 8th May 1213. The two friars then set out for the Porziuncola.

It was in these journeys, up and down the countryside, that Francis revealed the command he had over wild creatures. Once when numerous birds flocked round him, he told them they should praise their Creator 'for he has given you a dwelling in the purity of the air.' In one of his places of retreat, a falcon used to disturb him with its cries until he bade it keep quiet when he was at prayer. At Gubbio he tamed a ravening wolf. Many other instances could be mentioned of this power and it has caught the attention of many who have over-sentimentalized an aspect that Francis himself thought of as incidental to the religious faith too often ignored by these emotionalists.

He had, too, the gift of healing; many examples could be given, but it is difficult in dealing with miracle stories of the saints to discover the core of truth that has become enwrapped with later embellishments, and, in our sceptical age, we ask for more detailed diagnoses and for subsequent medical histories. What cannot be doubted is that the mere presence of Francis brought comfort and courage to many sufferers who were led to contemplate the sufferings of Our Lord and so be the better able to endure their own conditions.

The gift of the remote refuge of La Verna seems to have quickened the struggle between two conflicting inclinations with which Francis had to contend all his life. On the one hand was his intense desire to get away alone, or with two or three close companions, to some secluded place where they could pray and meditate; on the other was the call to evangelisation, of bringing to the people the Gospel message of repentance and reconciliation. He had in mind two kinds of friars; those who were more active in the world, and those who chose to live as hermits or with a few brethren and so keep the chain of prayer unbroken. Which course should he himself follow? The indications are that his own choice would have been the second of these ways of serving God. There was a third course; when any of the friars were wearied with much wandering and preaching they could withdraw for a while to some secluded retreat and refresh their spiritual lives in prayer and medtation far from the hubbub of the world.

When he got back to the Porziuncola from his northern journey, the conflict became acute. In his distraction — for even in prayer he could get no clear guidance — he sent his beloved companion Masseo first to Sister Clare and then to Brother Sylvester, the priest, who was in solitary retreat at that time. On his return Masseo reported that both were sure that Francis' duty was to save souls by his preaching. This came to him as the answer to his problem, and he at once said, 'Let us set out in the name of God.'

6.

Cardinal Ugolino

His failure to get to Syria did not lessen Francis' desire to preach to the heathen. Some two years later he decided to go to Spain and preach his way southwards until he could cross to Morocco. One of his companions was Bernard of Quintavalle. He had been sent by Francis to Bologna; at first Bernard had been made a laughing-stock, but eventually he so won over his detractors that they came to reverence him as a holy man, so much so that he feared he would become proud; in his humility he fled the city and begged Francis to send others there to build on the foundation he had been able to lay. Unfortunately no details of the Spanish journey have been recorded save that Francis' health broke down. Several friaries in Spain have claimed him as their founder and there is a tradition that he went to the tomb of the Apostle to Santiago de Compostella, but there is no firm evidence for these claims. Francis took his illness to mean that this particular mission was not for him, and he returned to Italy.

Francis was summoned to the Fourth Lateran Council in 1215 at Rome. The main purpose of Pope Innocent III was to promote a new crusade and on this subject he preached with great fervour. He took as his theme a verse from Ezekiel (9:4), 'Go through the midst of Jerusalem and mark *Tau* on the foreheads of the men that sigh and mourn for all the abominations that are committed there.' He explained that *tau* was the last letter of the Hebrew alphabet and took the shape of the cross without the projecting piece on which Pilate had the titulua affixed. (**T** *crux commissa*, St Anthony's Cross). These words struck home to Francis and ever afterwards he used the tau-cross as his sign. The Council did useful work in urging reforms that were needed especially in the Monastic Orders where local autonomy had led to abuses; triennial chapters of the Benedictines and Austin canons were to be held to issue statutes and to appoint visitors to see that these were observed. Regulations were also made for the selection of bishops and for the appointment of priests. This emphasis on regulation and discipline was to have its effect on the Fratres Minores who had been allowed to go their own way. It was also determined that any new penitential fraternities must in future be encouraged to enter an existing order, and that, in any case, no new Rules could be allowed. In these and other ways the Fourth Lateran Council was a landmark in church history. The decree on new Orders did not affect the Franciscans as the first Rule (if indeed it could be called that) drawn up by Francis had had the Pope's verbal approval, but it did affect Dominic (1170-1221), a Castilian, who was at the Council. His purpose was to form a group of trained priests who could effectively combat heresy. He himself was an Austin Canon and when he was told he must take one of the existing Rules for the Order of Preachers, he chose that of St Augustine.

Dominic and Francis met by chance in the streets of Rome during the Council. Dominic knew of the rapid spread of the Fratres Minores and he recognised Francis as a kindred spirit when he declared 'You are my comrade and we will run together. Let us stand together and no enemy shall overcome us'. Yet the two men were unlike one another in some significant ways. Dominic, who was some ten years older than Francis, and died four years before him, had been a religious from boyhood and had been a priest for fifteen years. His purpose, as has been noted, was to combat heresy by fully competent priests who could meet their opponents on an intellectual level. This meant a primary insistence on polemics and scholarship and the Dominicans played an important part in the revival of learning of the twelfth and thirteenth centuries, culminating in the work of their own Thomas Aquinas (d.1274). The attitude of Francis to learning was different. Priests, scholars and students were among those who followed him, but, it can safely be said that a preliminary requirement was that they should get rid of their books for the benefit of the poor. Francis objected to the ownership of books because it infringed the basic rule of poverty. The Gospels, Missals and Breviaries were Common property. 'Friars,' he said, 'should possess nothing except their habit with a cord and breeches, and if they are forced of necessity they may wear sandals.' He feared too that a love of books could become an obsession and result in acquisitiveness. A young brother once asked him if he could have a psalter. Francis said, 'After you have a psalter, you will desire and have a breviary. Then you will sit in your chair like a great prelate and say to your brother, "Bring me my breviary."' He admitted that he himself had at one time to resist the temptation to own books. One of his sayings was, 'There are so many who rise into knowledge, but he shall be blessed who makes himself barren for the love of God.' On one occasion when a poor woman came to the Porziuncola asking for alms, Francis looked round for something to give her that she could sell for bread; all he could find was the only copy of the Gospels the friars possessed; so he gave her that. We do not know what experience lay behind his attidude towards scholarship; had he listened to sermons by learned theologians that were unintelligible to the hearers? The main reason was probably his desire that the friars should use language that ordinary folk could understand and not confuse them with finely spun notions. Dominic was concerned with heretics and therefore his preachers had to be trained in polemics so that they could meet argument with argument. Francis feared that the pride of learning could remove the preacher into regions of thought where the uninstructed could not follow him. That he himself had a sure insight of the meaning of scripture is shown by the following incident. A doctor of divinity, a Dominican, quoted a text from Ezekiel and said, 'I have heard an exposition of this text by several wise men', but he was still puzzled. Francis told him how he understood the verse. Afterwards the Dominican said to some of his fellows, 'The theology of this man, founded on purity and contemplation is a flying eagle, while our science crawls on its belly on the earth.' Francis was not to see the day when Franciscan theologians were to be among the leading scholars at the universities, nor that a boy of five when Francis died would enter the Order and, as St Bonaventure, be declared a doctor of the church.

It was suggested to Dominic and Francis that worthy friars should be eligible as bishops. The argument put forward was persuasive.

'In the primitive church the pastors and prelates were poor, and men fervent in charity, not greed. Why therefore should we not make bishops of your friars, who should prevail over all others for a document and example?'

Both resisted this idea. Francis said,

'My brethren are called Minors for this reason, that they should not presume to become greater. For their vocation teaches them to remain lowly, and to imitate the footsteps of the humility of Christ, that hereby at last they may be exalted more than others in the sight of the saints. For if you would that they bring forth fruit in the Church of God, hold and keep them in the state of their calling, and if they strive for high things, cast them down violently to the ground, and never permit them to rise to any prelacy.'
(*Speculum Perfectionis,* XLIII)

Nonetheless the time was to come when Franciscans and Dominicans were to be bishops, cardinals and even popes.

As they were leaving on this occasion, Dominic asked Francis for the rope that he used as a girdle; this was granted reluctantly and Dominic 'from that time forth devoutly wore it.'

Francis's instinct was to let the Order grow by its own nature and its effective response to the world's needs. In the early years he would admit postulants like Guy of Cortona if he was satisfied of their true intentions. There were no formal vows. Admission, refusal and expulsion were at his will, but this direct personal control became impracticable as the numbers increased. A sluice-gate had been raised and the waters came flooding through. As he tramped the countryside (how many thousands of miles did he walk barefooted?) Francis would, of course, get to know the brothers he met, but this, within a few years, could not be done; there were too many of them. We do not know how postulants were accepted when Francis himself could no longer talk with each individual. In such a multitude, as in all human groupings, there must have been the awkward and self-assertive ones and the failures; how could discipline be kept so that the original simplicity was not lost? Such problems were bound to rise and, those with tidy minds, must have been disturbed. Most of us need, and, indeed, welcome guidance and direction; we doubt our own powers and are more at ease in an organised society. The friars all looked to Francis for this kind of help, but there was the practical difficulty of getting into touch with him, or even knowing where he was at any time.

Francis spent the winter of 1215-16 moving about Umbria and in July 1216 he was at the deathbed of Innocent III in Perugia. He was succeeded within a few days by Honorius, who, during the eleven years of his rule was to do much to promote the Franciscans and Dominicans as well as accomplishing important reforms within the Church. It had been arranged that the Porziuncola should be consecrated on the 2nd August. There was no thought yet of building a great church such as the present Santa Maria degli Angeli which was not begun until three hundred and fifty years later. The Porziuncola remained the small, plain chapel in the woods. While meditating on the coming consecration, Francis was inspired to beg the Pope that a plenary indulgence, a full pardon, should be granted to all who at any time visited the Little Portion after sacramental confession and with true contrition. The Pope objected that such a grant would be contrary to the custom of the Church. 'My Lord,' said Francis, 'what I ask is not from myself but from the Lord Jesus Christ.' As so often, it was difficult to resist an appeal by Francis. 'It is my will,' said the Pope, 'that you have what you ask.' The cardinals were astonished by this decision, and pointed out that such an indulgence would detract from that granted to the Crusaders. So the Pope limited the Pardon to the anniversary of the day of consecration. Seven bishops were present on that great occasion.

Perhaps it was when he asked for the indulgence that Francis preached before the Pope and the Cardinals. It is said that Cardinal Ugolino 'was in an agony of suspense, praying to God with all his might that the simplicity of the blessed man might not be despised.' He need not have worried. The same report tells us that,

> 'such was the fervour of his spirit as he spoke that, unable to contain himself for joy, as he uttered the words with his mouth he moved his feet as if dancing, not as in wantonness, but as glowing with the fire of Divine love; not provoking laughter, but extorting tears of grief. For many of them were pricked at the heart as they wondered at God's grace and the steadfastness of the man.' (*Celano*, I, para. 71).

The Porziuncola had become the home-ground of the

Fratres Minores. It was their abiding retreat where they could renew their sense of spiritual brotherhood with their founder and their brethren. Soon the custom was established, but when is not known, of as many as possible gathering there at Whitsun and Michaelmas, though the first was the more important. Out of what were at first informal reunions, developed the more formal Chapters; this was in accordance with the decrees of the Lateran Council. Plans could then be made for extending their apostolate. At the Chapter held in 1217, for instance, it was decided to divide the field into six provinces each under a Minister whose position, as Francis saw it, was not that of a ruler but of the mother of a household. He himself would not accept any office, not even that of leader. Peter Catanii became his Vicar or Minister-General. When the brethren separated Francis said to them,

'In the name of the Lord, go two and two on the way humbly and decently, and especially with strict silence from the dawn till past the hour of tierce (9 a.m.) praying the Lord in your hearts, and let not idle and useless words be so much as named amongst you. For though you walk, let your conversation be as humble and seemly as if you were in a hermitage or in a cell. For wherever we are and walk, we may always have our cell with us. For Brother Body is our cell; and our soul is the hermit, who remains in his cell, to pray to God and to meditate on Him. Whence if the soul does not remain in quiet in its cell, little profits the Religious a cell made with hands.'

He decided that he would go to France.

'In the name of Our Lord Jesus Christ and of the glorious Virgin Mary His Mother, and of all saints, I choose the province of France in which is a Catholic folk, especially because amongst all other Catholics they show great reverence to the Body of Christ, wherefore I shall converse with them most willingly.' (*Speculum Perfectionis*, LXV)

But once more his plans were to be hindered.

Masseo was his companion on this journey to France, but at Florence they found the papal legate for central and northern Italy, Cardinal Ugolino dei Conti, a nephew of Innocent III and, like him, a lawyer. He was perhaps thirty years older than Francis and outlived him fifteen years, and, as Pope Gregory IX, canonized him. They must have met in Rome on several occasions for there are indications that Francis went there more frequently than the records tell us, and they met at Perugia when Honorius succeeded Innocent. Ugolino was a devout priest who had an affection for Francis and fully appreciated the significance of his mission; Francis returned this esteem. There were, however, marked differences in their outlooks. By his training and natural inclination, Ugolino was an advocate of order and discipline and he could see that there were dangers in allowing some thousands of friars to wander about with no other guidance or control than the words of Francis who had just refused to be their authoritative head. Here was a problem that called for delicate handling. There was need to move cautiously between Francis's deep-rooted fears that rules and regulations might obstruct the free movement of the spirit, and the growing desire amongst the friars for effective direction. Fortunately, Ugolino had the necessary prudence to go one step at a time. At Florence he persuaded Francis not to go to France; he pointed out how desirable it was for Francis to be at hand when problems arose about the Fratres Minores. Francis objected that it was not seemly that he should send his brethren to other countries while he himself stayed in Italy and had no share in their risks and privations, but he gave way to the Cardinal's wishes and remained at home. Francis was impressed by the talks he had with the Cardinal. The Order's Protector, Cardinal John of St. Paul, had recently died and Francis, true to his determination to work with the Church's approval, asked that Cardinal Ugolino should take the friars under his care as

Protector; the Pope agreed to this suggestion.

It was during one of his visits to Rome that Francis came to know the Lady Giacoma, the widow of a patrician. She was left with two infant sons and with the responsibilities of great estates. How she came to consult Francis is not known, but he became, in effect, her spiritual director, and, under his guidance, she used her wealth in the service of the poor. He probably lodged with her when he was in Rome. He once said, 'There are only two women whose faces I should recognize if I looked at them.' They were Sister Clare and the Lady Giacoma.

The groups of friars who went to foreign countries had varied fortunes. It proved possible to get a footing in France, Spain and Portugal, but they were driven out of Germany, Hungary and neighbouring lands.

> 'They were expelled in the fear that they might prove to be infidels, for that, albeit the said Lord Innocent III had sanctioned their Order, and Rule, yet had he not confirmed it by his letters, for which reason the brethren endured many trials from clerics and laymen. Wherefore the brethren were compelled to flee from divers provinces, and thus straitened and afflicted, sometimes even robbed and beaten by thieves, they returned with great bitterness of spirit unto the Blessed Francis.' (*Three Companions*, XVI)

In addition to the lack of written credentials, the friars were hampered by their ignorance of the local languages. French and perhaps Spanish were spoken by some of them, but no one could speak German. It is impossible to convey through interpreters the true fervour of the evangelist. They learned from this set-back; when, for instance, in 1224 a party of nine went to England, three of their number were of English birth. No doubt after this initial reverse Cardinal Ugolino was all the more convinced that the Order must be put on a canonical basis. One of his early measures was to get papal letters issued to the bishops commending the friars to their protection. This was against the wish of Francis, and this opposition he maintained to the end and stated clearly in his Testament. He had earlier said:

'I wish by perfect humility and reverence first to convert the prelates who, when they shall see our holy life and humble reverence towards them, shall beseech you to preach and convert the people, and they shall call them to the preaching better than your privileges which would lead you into pride.'

7.

Brother Leo

OUR knowledge of St. Francis is largely based on the recollections of his close companions, especially those of Brother Leo. His writings have not survived but they were used in the early compilations, and they give us the most authentic impression of the personality and ideals of Francis.

When Brother Leo joined the Order he was already a priest and he may have been the most literate of the early brothers. It is interesting to compare the handwritings of Francis and Leo. They are both shown in the precious parchment known as the 'Blessing of Leo', of which more will be said in its place. Francis wrote in the large characters of one who is not a ready writer. Leo wrote with the neat script of one who is accustomed to the pen. This skill is displayed also in the breviary he made for Sister Clare.

Perhaps none of the friars came closer to the mind and heart of Francis as did Leo. How deeply he was influenced is shown in his strenuous opposition after the death of Francis to the building of a vast basilica to enshrine the saint's body. The Minister General, Elias, was the grand organiser of this ostentatious project. When he placed a marble vase near the building site for the contributions of the public, Leo and one or two like-minded companions went along and smashed it. For this Elias had them beaten by his servants, for he now had servants. But this is to jump ahead of time.

Two of Leo's treasured memories recorded in the *Fioretti*, (VIII, IX) are worth giving in full as they reveal so much of Francis's way of thinking.

The first tells us of what Francis meant by 'perfect joy.'

'When as Saint Francis was going one day from Perugia to Saint Mary of the Angels with Brother Leo in the spring tide, and the very bitter cold grievously tormented him, he called to Brother Leo that was going on before and said thus: "Brother Leo, though the Brothers Minor throughout all the world were great examples of sanctity and true edifying, nathless write it down and take heed diligently that not therein is perfect joy." And going on a little further, Saint Francis called a second time: "O Brother Leo, albeit the Brothers Minor should give sight to the blind, make straight the crooked, cast out devils, make the deaf to hear, the lame to walk, the dumb to speak, and (greater still) should raise them that have been dead a four days' space, write that not herein is perfect joy." And going on a little, he cried aloud: "O Brother Leo, if the Brother Minor should know all tongues and all sciences and all the Scriptures, so that he could prophesy and reveal not only things to come but also the secrets of consciences and souls, write that therein is not perfect joy." Going on yet a little further, Saint Francis called aloud once more: "O Brother Leo, thou little sheep of God, albeit the Brother Minor should speak with the tongue of angels, and know the courses of the stars and the virtues of herbs; and though all the treasures of earth were revealed unto him and he understood the virtues of birds, and of fishes, and of all animals, and of men, and of trees, and of stones and of roots, and of waters, write that not therein is perfect joy." And going on a little further, Saint Francis cried aloud: "Brother Leo, albeit the Brother Minor could preach so well as to turn all the infidels to the faith of Christ, write that not therein is perfect joy." And this manner of speech continuing for full two miles, Brother Leo with much marvel besought him, saying: "Father, I pray thee in the name of God that thou tell me, wherein is perfect joy."

And Saint Francis thus made answer: "When we come to Saint Mary of the Angels, all soaked as we are with rain and numbed with cold and besmirched with mud and tormented with hunger, and knock at the door, and the porter comes in anger and says, 'Who are ye?' and we say: 'We be two of the brethren', and he says, 'Ye be no true men: nay ye be two rogues that gad about deceiving the world and robbing the alms of the poor; get ye gone': and thereat he shuts the door and makes us stand without in the snow and the rain, cold and a-hungered, till night-fall; if therewithal we patiently endure such wrong and such cruelty and such rebuffs without being disquieted and without murmuring against him: and with humbleness and charity bethink us that this porter knows us full well and that God makes him speak against us — Brother Leo, write that therein is perfect joy. And if we be instant in knocking and he come out full of wrath and drive us away as importunate knaves, with insults and buffetings, saying: 'Get ye gone hence, vilest of thieves, begone to the alms-house, for here ye shall find nor food nor lodging'; and if we suffer this with patience and with gladness and with love, O brother Leo, write that herein is perfect joy. If we still constrained by hunger, cold and night knock yet again and shout and with much weeping pray him for the love of God that he will but open and let us in, and he yet more enraged should say: 'These be importunate knaves, I will pay them well as they deserve, 'and should rush out with a knotty stick and taking us by the hood, throw us upon the ground and send us rolling in the snow and beat us with all the knots of the stick: if with patience and with gladness we suffer all these things, thinking on the pains of the blessed Christ, the which we ought to suffer for the love of Him: O Brother Leo, write that here and herein is perfect joy: then hear the conclusion of the whole matter, Brother Leo: Above all graces and gifts of the Holy Spirit, that Christ granteth to His beloved, is to overcome oneself, and willingly for the love of Christ endure pains and insults and shame and want; inasmuch as in all other gifts of God we may not glory, sith they are not ours but God's; whence saith the Apostle: What hast thou that thou hast not received of God? And if thou hast received it of Him, wherefore boastest thou thyself as if thou hadst it of thyself? But in the cross of tribulation and affliction we may boast, sith this is ours; and therefore saith the Apostle, I would not that I should glory save in the cross of our Lord Jesus Christ."'

Did Leo recall these words as he was being beaten by the servants of the Minister General?

The second of Leo's recollections describes a curious conflict in which he withstood Francis' will.

'It befell on a time in the beginning of the Order that Saint Francis was with Brother Leo in a place where they had not books to say the divine office withal; when the hour of matins came, said Saint Francis to Brother Leo: "Dear son, we have no breviary wherewith to say matins; but to the end that we may spend the time in praising God, I will speak and thou shalt answer as I shall teach thee: and take good heed that thou change not the words to other than I shall teach thee. I shall say thus: O Brother Francis, so many sins and evils hast thou done in the world that thou art deserving of hell; and thou, Brother Leo, shalt answer: Sooth is it thou meritest the lowest depth of hell." But Brother Leo with dove-like simplicity replied: "Right willingly, father; begin in the name of God." Then began Saint Francis to say: "So many sins and evils hast thou done in the world that thou art deserving of hell." And Brother Leo made answer; "God will work through thee so much good that thou wilt go to paradise." Quoth Saint Francis: "Nay, say not so, Brother Leo; but when I shall say: Brother Francis, so many iniquities hast thou done against God that thou art worthy to be accursed to God, do thou answer thus: In very sooth art thou worthy to be set among the accursed ones." And Brother Leo replied: "Right willingly, father." Therewith Saint Francis with many tears and sighs and beating of the breast cried with a loud voice: "O my lord of heaven and earth, I have done against thee so many iniquities and so many sins that I am altogether worthy to be accursed of Thee"; and Brother Leo made answer: "O Brother Francis, God will do so unto thee that among the blessed shalt thou above all be blessed." And Brother Francis marvelling that Brother Leo answered to the contrary of what he had laid upon him, reproved him saying: "Wherefore dost thou not answer even as I teach? I command thee by holy obedience that thou answer as I shall teach thee. I shall say thus: O Brother, Francis, vile wretch", thinkest thou that God will have mercy on thee, seeing thou has committed so many sins against the Father of mercy and God of all consolation, that thou art not worthy to find mercy. And thou, Brother Leo, little sheep, wilt answer: In no wise art thou worthy to find mercy." But whereas Saint Francis said: "O Brother Francis, vile wretch" and the like, Brother Leo made answer: "God the Father, whose mercy is infinitely greater than thy sin, will show thee great mercy, and, more than this, will pour upon thee many graces." And this reply Saint Francis being sweetly angered and patiently disquieted, said unto Brother Leo: "And wherefore hast thou had the boldness to do against obedience, and now so many times hast answered to the contrary of that which I laid upon thee?" Replied Brother Leo right humbly and reverently: "God knows, father, that each time I set it in my heart to answer as thou didst bid me; but God makes me speak as it pleaseth Him and not as it pleaseth me." Whereat Saint Francis marvelled, and said to Brother Leo: "I pray thee most lovingly that this time thou answer as I have told thee." Replied Brother Leo: "Speak in the name of God, for of a surety will I this time answer as thou wishest." And Saint Francis weeping said: "O Brother Francis, vile wretch, thinkest thou that God will have mercy upon thee?" Replied Brother Leo: "Nay, rather, great grace shalt thou receive of God and He shall exalt thee and glorify thee for ever, for every one that humbleth himself shall be exalted, and naught other can I say since God speaketh through my mouth."

And thuswise in this humble strife, with many tears and much spiritual consolation, they kept watch until the day.'

8.

The Crusade

ON one occasion when he was to dine with Cardinal Ugolino, Francis first of all went round the neighbourhood begging for alms; the guests were already seated at table when he returned; he placed in front of him the food he had been given and he sent portions to the others. The Cardinal made no comment during the meal but afterwards he remonstrated with Francis for embarrassing him in such a fashion. Francis replied.

> 'Let those who are and shall be friars know that I hold it for greater consolation of soul and body to sit at the sorry table of the friars, and see before me the wretched alms which they beg from door to door for the love of the Lord God, than to sit at your table, or that of other lords, abundantly prepared with diverse dainties. For the bread of charity is holy bread which the praise and love of the Lord God sanctifies.' (*Speculum Perfectionis*, XXIII).

Had Francis on this occasion failed to show that courtesy which he valued so highly? His host was not one of the prelates who lived luxuriously. The Cardinal, we are told, 'was much edified.' This was but one instance of how Francis taught not only by words but by practical demonstration even at the risk of giving offence. Another incident of the same kind was when he rebuked some friars at Rieti who wished to celebrate the Christmas Feast. They had taken some care to lay out the table as neatly as they could, but there does not seem to have been any special food. When Francis saw how the table had been arranged, he went outside and, borrowing the staff and wallet of a beggar, returned in that guise. The friars, of course, knew him when he came in and begged alms of them. The Minister at once offered him his own share of 'the alms which the Lord hath given us.' Francis went to the fire and sat down on the floor to eat his portion. Afterwards he admonished them for having 'a table worshipfully and sumptuously laid out and not the table of poor religious who daily go from door to door for alms." So again he had dramatized the need for humility and poverty. Our sympathies may well be with the friars who, out of their slender resources, had contrived to mark the feast of Christ's Birth in a special manner, but, Francis told them, 'the feasts of the Lord and of the saints are rather honoured with the want and poverty by which those saints conquered heaven for themselves, than with the elegance and superfluity by which they be made distant from heaven." (*Speculum Perfectionis*, XX). Such incidents, and others could be given, show how inflexible Francis was in his pursuit of poverty.

As Protector of the Fratres Minors, Cardinal Ugolino was also concerned with the Poor Ladies of San Damiano and the convents that had been formed on the same principles. Sister Clare was as determined as Francis that the rule of poverty, of owning nothing, should be strictly observed. What of the building they occupied? the original small chapel and priest's house sufficed for the early days, but as numbers increased an extension was needed, but how could the Poor Ladies own property? Ugolino decided that any funds received for building should be held in the name of the Holy See. A similar expedient was used later when the friars settled in towns and needed some kind of permanent, though modest, quarters. The property was held by the Holy See on behalf of the friars. Francis was strongly opposed to the friars owning property; The Porziunculo was held on a nominal rent. Yet it might be said that he had broken his rule when he accepted La Verna by a deed of gift; however, as this was a wild and inhospitable place it was unlikely that anyone would covet it. Such problems were bound to arise as the numbers of the friars increased as they did very rapidly.

The Poor Ladies formed the Second Order. The origins of the Third Order remain obscure, but, at an early stage, laymen were anxious to be closely associated with the Fratres Minores. Francis wrote a 'Letter to the Faithful', probably about 1215, in which he showed how people active in the world could yet live in the spirit of the Order. He urged them to go to Confession regularly, to receive the Blessed Sacrament as often as possible, to be generous in almsgiving, to fast and be temperate in eating, to visit churches and reverence the clergy, and to be simple, humble and pure in their lives. The influence of this Third Order grew with the years and it would be difficult to exaggerate its power for good during the past seven centuries.

Cardinal Ugolino attended the Pentecost Chapters after his appointment; it was his custom when in sight of the chapel to dismount and to proceed bare-footed, and, at times, he wore the friars' habit. The Chapter of 1219 became known as the Chapter of Mats because the several thousand friars who had gathered there lived in brushwood huts they themselves put up. At the outset there was a disturbing incident. Francis had been away for some time and when he arrived at the Porziuncola, he was horrified to see that a hall of stone had been built in the grounds; this was so entirely contrary to the ideal of fundamental poverty, that he climbed on to the roof, and with the help of some friars, began to dismantle it. One of the town guard which was there to control the crowds who had gathered to see the friars, intervened and explained that the hall had been put up by the Commune of Assisi to whom it belonged. Francis at once gave up his attempt at demolition. The Commune, proud of the town's association with Francis, had decided to put up the building for the convenience of the friars and further arranged for its upkeep. It was a kindly thought. This incident was one indication of the undertone of discontent that marked this Chapter. Perhaps 'discontent' is too strong a word. Some of the friars felt the need for stricter regulation in

the conduct of their affairs; they were not disgruntled or
intractable; the good of the Order was uppermost in their
minds. In their experience up and down the country and
beyond Italy and especially in the towns, they had had to face
problems which, they felt, Francis did not appreciate. So they
approached the Cardinal. They put their case in this way: 'My
lord, we wish you would persuade Brother Francis to follow the
counsel of wise brethren and to allow himself now and then to
be led by them.' They explained that what they had in mind
was something on the lines of the Rules drawn up by St
Augustine, St Benedict and St Bernard so that they could 'live
in order.' The Cardinal passed on this plea to Francis who
called the brethren together and said to them:

> 'My brethren, my brethren! The Lord has called me by the
> way of simplicity and humility, and this way hath He
> pointed out to me in truth for myself and for them who are
> willing to believe me and imitate me. Wherefore I will not
> that you name to me any other Rule, neither of St Benedict
> nor of St Augustine nor of St Bernard, nor any other
> manner of living beside that which the Lord in His mercy
> hath shown and given me. The Lord told me that He willed
> me to be poor and foolish in this world, and that He willed
> not to lead us by any way other than by that knowledge. But
> with this learning and wisdom of yours, may the Lord
> confound you, and I trust in the wardens of the Lord that
> through them God will punish you, and that you will return
> to your vocation for all your fault-finding, whether you will
> or no.' (*Speculum Perfectionis*, LXVIII)

There is a touch of anger in those words; the desire expressed by
the friars struck at the heart of Francis's purpose and ideals. It
must be kept in mind, as has been said, 'he was a poet bearing
witness to the vision he saw.'

The Cardinal did not press the question at that Chapter, but
he must have been strengthened in his belief that there was

need for a better organisation of the Order's affairs; no steps were taken at that time to meet the complaints. The main work of the Chapter was to arrange for the friars to set out for foreign countries. Francis himself decided to lead a mission to the Moslems in Egypt who were facing the armies of the Fifth Crusade. Ugolino had persuaded Francis not to go to France two years earlier; he probably raised no objections to this eastern mission as it was connected with the Crusade.

The Fifth Crusade was a muddled affair that brought little credit to anyone. This time the attack on the Moslem power was to be from Egypt; the infamous sack of Constantinople in 1204 by the armies of the Fourth Crusade had closed that route for future attempts. There had been little response when Pope Honorius appealed to the kings of Europe to take part in a new Crusade; the official leader was John of Brienne, an obscure knight at the French court. The first objctive was Damietta, a fortified town at the eastern end of the Nile Delta. The Christian forces were rent by personal rivalries among the leaders and by national jealousies. The papal legate, Cardinal Pelagius, had his own views on strategy and these rarely won the assent of the fractious leaders.

Before he left on his mission, Francis appointed two Vicars to act for him; Matthew of Narni was to remain at the Porziuncola, while Gregory of Naples was to move about to keep in touch with as many friars as possible. Francis sailed from Ancona in June 1219 with a dozen companions including Peter Catanii and Illuminato. There had been some competition to go with him and, it is said, Francis asked a child to pick out those who were to form the mission. They travelled by way of Cyprus and Acre and thence to Egypt where they joined the besiegers of Damietta. Francis was bitterly shocked at the licentiousness of the soldiers over whom the leaders had little control. He warned them that there could be no blessing on their arms while they behaved so shamelessly. This was borne out when, at the end of August, the Crusaders were defeated. In fact it was they who needed the mission, not the Moslems.

In the lull after the rout of the Crusaders, Francis begged Cardinal Pelagius to let him seek an interview with Sultan al-Kamil. Permission was granted though the Cardinal may have thought, as others did, that the idea was hare-brained. So Francis with Illuminato as his companion crossed no-man's land; the outposts stopped him; indeed it was surprising that the friars were not immediately killed. The soldiers probably stayed their hands because they thought these two shabby, bare-footed Christians were demented, 'touched by God', and therefore, according to Moslem ideas, not to be harmed. So they were brought before the Sultan who far from being a savage barbarian, as he was pictured in the West, was highly-civilised and well-bred. The Moslems tolerated Christians as people of the Book, and rarely persecuted them. The Sultan listened courteously to Francis's exposition of the teaching of Christ; perhaps he did not know that the Moslems accept Jesus Christ as a true prophet. Francis proposed an ordeal by fire, but the Sultan had no wish to stir up public controversy; he offered Francis valuable gifts but these were refused and he and his companion were escorted with honour back to the Christian lines.

Francis remained with the army until Damietta was taken in November 1219; the treatment of the captives, many of whom were sold into slavery, and the looting by the soldiers and their unbridled license disgusted Francis. The preaching of the friars made little impact but some clerics (we should call them army chaplains) decided to join the Order and went with Francis and his companions back to Acre where they were met by Brother Elias who had a year earlier been put in charge of the province of Syria. Francis spent some months preaching in Syria and in visiting the Holy Places. There are many gaps in our knowledge of his life, but none is more regrettable than our lack of knowledge of his pilgrimage to the Holy Land. It has just been noted that the Moslems did not molest Christians; the harmless pilgrim shared the risks of the native population of attacks by brigands and of being caught up in local wars, but usually he was allowed to move about freely. It may be noted that the Moslems always respected the Church of the Holy Sepulchre in Jerusalem. The idealism and romanticism of the Crusades perished in the wholesale massacres and the ruthless power-seeking that marked their history.

Brother Stephen of Narni was waiting for Francis when he eventually returned to Acre; he had been sent by some of the friars to beg Francis to hurry back as the two Vicars had imposed new rules and had ill-treated those who had refused to conform. One of the rules was on fasting. It was now laid down by the Vicars that friars were to fast on Mondays as well as upon days already agreed upon, but Francis had always left a wide discretion to the brothers. Another ruling was that friars were not to eat meat at any time. It so happened that Francis read this rule when he was about to have a meal in which meat had been included; so he said, 'We will eat what is set before us according to the Gospel.' Francis with Elias and Peter Catanii, Caesar of Speyer, who had been one of the preachers of the Crusade, and their companions, took passage as soon as possible, for Venice; this was probably in the autumn of 1220.

9.

The New Rule

WHEN he landed in Italy, Francis was a sick man. He had contracted conjunctivitis and probably suffered from malaria, and there were intestinal disorders beyond the diagnosis of contemporary medicine. He was to suffer much pain and distress during the few years of life left to him. After resting at Venice, he made his way to Bologna, and because of his infirmities, he rode an ass. The minister at Bologna was John (or Peter) de Stacia who was a doctor of laws. He had built a house for the friars. Francis was angry both because he did not want the brethren to own property and because, as we have seen, he was opposed to the kind of studies pursued at Bologna; this building seemed designed as a house of studies. He refused to enter it and ordered the friars as well as the sick who were being tended there, to quit the building at once. When he heard of this, Cardinal Ugolino declared that the house belonged to him and he had lent it to the friars. Francis gave way, but he still insisted that the friars should not think of themselves as settled anywhere permanently, 'to the end that everything might sing of pilgrimage and exile', as one of the sick friars of Bologna reported.

While Francis was absent, the Pope had imposed a novitiate of one year on the Order in line with what was customary in other Orders. Francis did not like this but, Rome had spoken so he accepted the ruling. The new Constitutions drawn up by the Vicars were a very different matter. They were in part based upon those made by Cardinal Ugolino for the Poor Nuns of San Damiano; he regarded the privilege of absolute poverty granted by Pope Innocent to Clare as peculiar to her and her community, but other convents, founded on the same principles, needed, he insisted, some property to maintain them.

The action of the Vicars, who may have believed a rumour that Francis had died in the East, in insisting on obedience to their behests all but disrupted the Order; those who refused to obey were subjected to severe penances, and the most stubborn were expelled. Only the return of Francis prevented immediate disaster.

When Francis and his companions got back to the Porziuncola, Peter Catanii resumed his position as Vicar or Minister-General. When he died a few months later (10th March 1221 — the inscribed stone for his tomb is preserved in the wall of the Porziuncola), Francis chose Brother Elias to take his place. It was to prove a momentous appointment. The enigma of his personality cannot be solved. Whatever view we take of his later conduct, it should be remembered that Francis chose him (though Cardinal Ugolino may have been consulted) and had confidence in him, and was content to leave the direction of affairs more and more in his Vicar's control. Elias, on his part, was most solicitous for Francis's well-being during his decline in health. Elias in his own person summed up the acute problems that were to beset the Order. Francis was still able to make occasional preaching journeys, but he spent more of his time in retreat with two or three companions.

It was probably at Cardinal Ugolino's request that Francis revised the first Rule. The Order was, in fact, in an anomalous position; the Rule had only the verbal approval of Innocent III and, any Order was required to have its Rule canonically recognised in writing by the Holy See; this condition was reinforced by the decrees of the Fourth Lateran Council. Ugolino had seen that this was done for the later foundations of the Poor Ladies. It must have been with some misgivings and a heavy heart that Francis accepted this charge. His own view was simple, some thought even naïve, but, if so it was the naïvety of the Gospels. He held that anyone who simple-heartedly accepted the rule of poverty in the following of Christ should be admitted to the Fratres Minores, and, thereafter, be left free to the guidance of the Holy Spirit.

To carry out his task he sought a rock cavern in the mountains west of Rieti, now known as the heritage of Colombo. As his companions he took with him the beloved Brother Leo and Brother Bonizzo of Bologna, of whom little is known save that he was a frequent companion of Francis in those last years. When the revised Rule had been written down, no doubt by Brother Leo, it was taken to the Porziuncola, but when, later on inquiries were made about it, Elias declared that it had been mislaid. Was this intentional? Some of the Ministers may have read it, or were worried as to the line it was thought that Francis would take. 'We fear,' they told Elias, 'lest he make the new Rule so harsh that we may not observe it. Therefore we will that you go to him and say that we will not be bound to that Rule; let him make it for himself and not for us.' By 'harsh' they did not mean 'rigorous' but too insistent on absolute poverty which they found restricted them too much. This was blunt speaking and surely wanting in respect. They asked Elias to put their view to Francis, but the Vicar, prudently, would only do so if they went with him. This confrontation gives us the rare sight of a really angry Francis of Assisi. He declared that the Rule must be observed 'to the letter, without a gloss, without a gloss!' He added that those who would not obey it should leave the Order. 'Then the Ministers, looking upon one another, went back confused and terrified.' So Francis set to work to produce another copy or version of his Rule. Our information is too scrappy to provide a connected and detailed account, such as we should like to have, of this process of Rule-making, nor can we compare versions since only the final one is extant. How far were the Ministers consulted after their rebuff? Was the Rule submitted to the Chapter? Such questions must remain unanswered, but it seems clear that the Ministers objected to the retention of the clause, 'The Rule and life of the brothers is this: namely, to live in obedience, in chastity and without property. 'It was the 'without property' that stuck. The friars had found that they could not avoid, certainly in towns, having somewhere to call their own where people could come to them and where they could shelter and care for the needy. Francis had objected to the building at Bologna even though it was in part a hospital. His own spiritual progress had been assured by his communion, his 'converse', with Lady Poverty; it had been a hard struggle for him to give up the amenities and pleasures he had enjoyed as the son of a rich man, and it was not until he made the renunciation that he had gained peace of spirit. He was unshakenly convinced that those who chose to follow him must take the same path. The Ministers were not lusting after the flesh-pots; they were not asking for easy living; they accepted the rule of personal poverty though some would have liked books; but they had to face the meeting of communal needs if the friars were to be anything else but roving evangelists who did not settle anywhere long enough to consolidate their work. Had Francis ever thought of the friars being settled in towns and establishing permanent ministries? We can sympathise with Francis's determination to preserve what he regarded as a fundamental principle, but we can also understand the problems the Ministers had to face. It is not surprising that tempers were frayed. There are few sadder spectacles in the world than that of good men at loggerheads.

Francis himself took the draft Rule to Rome. We cannot tell how far the Cardinal and the Pope modified some of the provisions, but, in all essentials, it reflects the spirit of Francis. The strict rule of travelling with neither purse nor staff was omitted; here can be seen perhaps, the influence of the Cardinal in response to the objections made by the Ministers. Whether the new Rule was wholeheartedly acceptable to the

Ministers may be doubted; indeed, in later years, Elias declared that he had not made profession of it. This may have been technically true, for, as far as we know, the friars were not required to renew their profession when the new Rule, which is still operative, was solemnly approved by Pope Honorius on the 29th March 1223.

10.

La Verna

WITH the Rule approved by the Pope, a change came over Francis's life. From then he took no active part in the government of the Order; he had no liking for controlling others and no wish for power over them. So he gave himself to his preaching but he was more and more drawn to the life of prayer and meditation with a few companions in one or other of the mountain retreats or hermitages that had been given to the friars by landowners who held them in honour and treasured the opportunity of serving them.

Francis was still a seeker, still trying to plumb the depths of Christ's teaching; still trying to perfect his own spiritual life. His religious thought was Christ-centred, Gospel-centred. His recorded words and his few writings are mosaics of verses from the Gospels; that he did not show any special devotion to Our Lady is the more surprising when one considers the prestige she enjoys in the Church and especially in Italy. During his last two or three years, Francis concentrated his thoughts even more than before on the life of Christ and especially on the Passion.

When Francis and his companions left Rome towards the end of 1223, they made their way to one of his favourite localities, the Lago di Piedilucco, a few miles north of Rieti with Poggio Bustone to the east and Greccio to the south-west. Giovanni da Vellita, a tertiary who owned land round Greccio, had given the friars a 'place' or 'station' there and, up in the mountain, a rock-cell. It was here that Francis decided to spend Christmas. Perhaps memories came to him of his visit to the Holy Land and to Bethlehem, and he thought of a new way of marking the feast; once again his instinct led him to give visible expression to the faith as an aid to the devotion of ordinary folk. He called Giovanni to him and asked him to prepare a stable with a manger (presepio) and have an ox and an ass in readiness. Word was then sent round for friars and people to assemble at Greccio on Christmas Eve — they came with torches to the stable and there saw the manger full of hay with the ox and ass nearby. The only record reads:

'The night was lit up as the day and was delightsome to men and beasts. The people came, and at the new Mystery rejoiced with new rejoicings. The woodland rang with voices, the rocks made answer to the jubilant throng. The brethren sang, yielding due praises to the Lord, and all that night resounded with jubilation. The solemnities of Mass were celebrated over the manger and the priest enjoyed a new consolation. The Saint of God with a sonorous voice chanted the holy Gospel — an earnest, sweet, clear and loud-sounding voice. Then he preached to the people who stood around, and uttered mellifluous words concerning the birth of the poor King and the little town of Bethlehem.' (*Celano*, I. para. 86).

This does not give all the details one would wish to have of this first Christmas crib. There is no suggestion, for instance, of the actual representation of the babe. We are told:

'A vision of wondrous efficacy was seen by a certain man; for in the manger he saw a little child lying lifeless, to whom the Saint of God seemed to draw near and (as it were) to rouse the child from the lethargy of sleep.'

Nor is there any reference to Mary and Joseph and the shepherds. It would seem to have been just the manger filled with hay and the actual ox and ass; in their presence we can see the mind of Francis. Since then the crib has become part of the Christmas Feast, but, alas, modern stage effects too often rob it of its first simplicity. Perhaps it would be too much to hope to see the ox and the ass beside the altar!

The little company of friars left Greccio in the spring of 1224 and were at the Porziuncola in time for the Pentecost Chapter. It was then that it was decided to send a mission to England under Angellus of Pisa. Francis with Leo (Il pecorello di Dio, God's little sheep, as Francis called him), Angelo Tancredi, Masseo, Ruffino, Illuminato, and Sylvester the priest, then set out for La Verna, fifty miles or more northwards. They arrived there early in August. It was Francis' first visit. He had earlier sent some friars to prospect and their report had enthused him for this mountain given by Orlando. They reported on its wild seclusion with its masses of fissured rock and its woods of beech and pine. This was just the place, Francis decided, best suited for the purpose he had in mind — to pass an autumn Lent or fast from the Assumption (15th August) to the Feast of St Michael (29th September) in prayer and meditation. It is significant of his strong sense of fellowship that Francis did not propose going into retreat by himself; he wanted to be solitary yet, at the same time, to have his brethren within call as it were. Orlando was overjoyed when he heard of the coming of Francis and the friars, and he hastened to welcome them and to assure them that they need not worry about their physical needs as he would supply those. He constructed a small oratory which was dedicated to Santa Maria degli Angeli, thus linking it with the Porziuncola.

Francis wished to be out of hearing of his companions; he stood some way off and called to Leo who could still hear him, so Francis went farther away and they tried the test again until they could not hear one another. A beech tree stood at the chosen place, and there the friars made a brushwood shelter for Francis. Only Leo was allowed to come to him once a day with bread and water. After a time, Francis wanted even greater seclusion and he chose a ledge of rock above a chasm; a tree trunk was thrown across as a bridge, and only Leo was allowed to cross it; when he reached the bridge at the hour of Matins, he was to call out 'Domine, labia mea aperies', then, if Francis replied, Leo could go over, but if there was no reply he was to go away. The time was approaching when Francis was to attain that mystical knowledge of God that is rarely granted even to the most devout, and that cannot be communicated in words; attempted descriptions merely touch the fringe of the experience. As the days passed, Leo could sense that Francis was going through an agonising spiritual trial and then, when Francis failed to reply, Leo, in some trepidation , crossed the chasm. Francis was not in his shelter, but a little way off, in an ecstasy of prayer. Leo began to withdraw as silently as he could, but he was heard. Francis mildly rebukd him, but told him something of his experience; he had been shown, he said, the knowledge and understanding of his own lamentable vileness and misery, but he had also been shown the knowledge and understanding of the Creator. They then went to the little oratory and Francis bade Leo to open the Gospels at random; the page told of the Passion of Christ; twice more Leo opened the book, and each time it was at the story of the Passion. From this Francis knew what must be the subject of his meditations in his solitary retreat. Did he recall that earlier divination when Bernard of Quintavalle became his first companion?

His supreme experience came at the time of the Feast of the Holy Cross, the 14th September. Here it is best to quote the words of Thomas of Celano who recorded what the companions had told him.

'He saw in a vision of God a man like a seraph having six wings, standing over him with hands outstretched and feet joined together, fixed to a cross. Two wings were raised above his head, two were spread out for flight, and two veiled the whole body. Now, when the blessed servant of the Most High saw this, he was filled with exceeding great wonder, but he could not understand what this vision might mean. Yet he rejoiced greatly and was filled with vehement delight at the benign and gracious look wherewith he saw that he was regarded by the seraph, whose beauty far exceeded all estimation; but the crucifixion, and the bitterness of the seraph's suffering smote him altogether with fear. Thus he arose, so to speak, sorrowful and glad; and joy and grief alternated in him. He anxiously pondered what this vision might portend, and his spirit labored sore to come at the understanding of it. And while he continued without any clear perception of its meaning, and the strangeness of the vision was perplexing his heart, marks of nails began to appear in his hands and feet, such as he had seen a little while before in the Man crucified who had stood over him.

His hands and feet seemed pierced in the midst by nails, the heads of the nails appearing in the inner part of the hands and in the upper part of the feet, and their points over against them. Now those marks were round in the inner side of the hands and elongated on the outer side, and certain small pieces of flesh were seen like the ends of nails bent and driven back, projecting from the rest of the flesh. So also the marks of nails were imprinted in his feet, and raised above the rest of the flesh. Moreover his right side, as it had been pierced by a lance, was overlaid with a scar, and often shed forth blood, so that his tunic and drawers were many times sprinkled with the sacred blood.' (*Celano*, I, paras 94-5).

That description, should be read and re-read carefully. Its precision carries conviction. The facts of this first recorded stigmatization could not be concealed from his most intimate

brethren, but, at first, it was only Leo who was fully aware of
the wounds for it was he who renewed the bandages that were
necessary to ease the pain and absorb the blood. There was an
especially close fellowship between Francis and Leo. Not only
had Leo been present in the early stage of Francis's ordeal,
but he himself at that time had been deeply distressed by a
spiritual temptation the nature of which is not known.
Francis, however, with his sensitive spirit, was aware that his
companion was suffering and he thought of a way to help him.
He wrote down these sentences from Scripture.

> 'The Lord bless thee and keep thee.
> The Lord show His face to thee and have mercy upon thee.
> The Lord turn His countenance to thee and give thee peace.'

Underneath these words he added,

> Brother Leo may our Lord bless thee.

At the bottom of the parchment he made a rough drawing of a
head (a lion?) and upon this the tau-cross.

On the other side of the parchment Francis had written a
doxology of his own composition.

> 'Thou alone art the holy Lord and God, doer of wonders.
> Thou art strong, thou art great, thou art high above all.
> Thou art mighty, holy Father, King of heaven and earth.
> Thou art Three and thou art One, the King of Kings.
> Thou art good, thou art all goodness, the highest good, Lord,
> one true God.
> Thou art love, thou art wisdom, thou art humility, patience
> and beauty.
> Thou art safety, peace and joy.
> Thou art our hope, thou art justice and equity, thou our riches
> and sufficiency.
> Thou art our refuge and our strength, thou art unfathomable,
> great and adorable goodness.'

This precious parchment is preserved in the basilica at Assisi.
On it Leo wrote an account of the circumstances. There is also
a letter to Brother Leo now kept at Spoleto. Perhaps it was
written after they got back to the Porziuncola.

> 'Brother Leo, your brother Francis sends you peace and
> greeting. I am telling you, as a mother tells her son, that all
> the things we talked about on the journey I can put into a
> few words of advice, so that you don't have to come to me
> for advice about everything; because my advice to you is
> that in whatever way you are pleasing the Lord God, and
> following his footsteps and his poverty, you are doing it
> with the blessing of the Lord God and in obedience to me.
> But if your spirit has any need of further consolation and
> you want to come to me, then, Leo, just come.' (*Writings*,
> pp. 146-9).

It was time to leave La Verna; Francis felt the call of the
mission field and of the Porziuncola and the brethren there.
The record made by Brother Masseo tells us of the parting.
This manuscript is now at the friary of La Verna.

> 'Our dearest father had decided to bid farewell to the holy
> mountain on 30th September, the Feast of St Jerome. My
> lord Orlando had sent up a beast for him to ride on, since,
> on account of the wounds on his feet, he could not walk.
> Early that morning he heard Mass as usual in the little
> chapel of Our Lady of the Angels. Then he summoned the
> brethren and commanded them under obedience: they
> were to remain lovingly together, to give themselves to
> prayer, and to recite their Office by day and by night.
> Then he commended to their care the holy mountain:
> never were the brethren, now or in the future, to use this
> mountain for any secular purpose: on the contrary, they
> were always to look upon it as a holy place, and he would
> bless quite specially those who lived here or looked after

the holy place reverently. To me he then said, "Brother Masseo, I want you to know that it is my desire that only good religious should live here — the best of my Order. Oh, Brother Masseo, what more can I say?"

Then he began to take his leave: "Farewell, Brother Masseo," he said, "Farewell. Farewell, farewell, Brother Angelo." And he said the same to Brother Sylvester and Brother Illuminato. Then he said, "Live in peace, my dearest sons, and God bless you. I am going away, but my heart stays with you. I am going with Brother Leo, the little sheep of God. I am going to Santa Maria degli Angeli, and I shall never come back. Now I must go, farewell, and love one another!"

So Francis on the ass and Leo on foot set out on their journey to the Porziuncola. As they passed through the villages and towns the people crowded to welcome them, but Francis, lost in his own thoughts after the strain of his experience on La Verna, barely noticed how much attention was being paid to him. It was not an easy journey. They stayed for the first night with the friars at the hermitage of Monte Casale; here Francis healed a brother who was an epileptic. Their next stop was at Città di Castello where they remained for several weeks; it may be that Francis was feeling exhausted. He healed a number of sick folk and he drove the devil out of a distraught woman.

When they left Castello they seem to have lost their way over the mountain they had to cross, for they became benighted and had to shelter as best they could among the rocks. Snow was falling and they had no fire. The owner of the ass complained of the hardships they had brought upon him, but Francis calmed him down and the man later declared that by just touching him, the saint had brought warmth and sleep. At daylight they were able to find their way and that evening they reached the Porziuncola where 'they were received by the brothers with exceeding joy and love.'

Francis took every precaution to keep the stigmatization a secret. Leo had known from the first, but others of the intimate circle of those last months, could not avoid seeing the wounds as, in his great physical weakness, they had to handle his body. It was inevitable that vague rumours spread beyond the Porziuncola, but Francis would not allow any pronouncement to be made.

Attempts have been made to explain away the stigmatization and even to deny that it could have taken place. It is incredible that those nearest and dearest to Francis should have invented a sign of Divine Grace of a nature that had not previously been recorded and one that was not among the accepted marks of sanctity. Moreover the carefully worded description just quoted given by Thomas of Celano is decisive; he based his life of St Francis on the evidence of 'faithful and approved witnesses', one of whom was certainly Leo. As Fr. Cuthbert wrote, 'After all, Celano wrote his *Legenda Prima* only two years or thereabouts after the saint's death, and there were many witnesses at hand who had seen the stigmata whilst the saint lay dead at the Porziuncola.'

11.

The Canticle of the Sun

WE cannot know with certainty in what state of mind and spirit Francis left Rome after the ratification of the Rule. He had preserved the essentials, but, in accordance with the wishes of the Pope and of Cardinal Ugolino he had made some modifications that must have distressed him. The Rule had not, it was true, become the strait-jacket that some had hoped it would be; that, at least, was some consolation. The attitude of the Ministers had angered him momentarily; it showed that some of the friars were thinking along lines that were contrary to his basic conception. There had also been disappointments. This is expressed by Thomas of Celano in some sentences that follow his account of the stigmatization.

> 'He had found some who agreed with him outwardly and disagreed with him inwardly, applauding him to his face and mocking him behind his back; who got credit for themselves and made him somewhat mistrustful of the upright.' (*Celano*, I., para. 96).

These words may have been influenced by the developments that came immediately after Francis's death, but they had been latent for several years and Francis was aware of the dangers and this must have saddened him.

Part of his purpose in going to La Verna, the farthest off of all their retreats, had been to seek divine reassurance in his mission. This he received in a unique form. As he told the brethren, the angel sent by God had comforted him, by this promise:

> 'I tell you in the name of God, that the profession of the

Order will never fail until the Day of Judgment, and there will be no sinner so great as not to find mercy with God, if with his whole heart he love your Order; ... Grieve not if in your Order you see certain that are not good brothers who do not observed the Rule as they should, and think not that thereby this Order will decline; for always many will be found in it that will perfectly observe the Gospel life of Christ and the purity of the Rule.' (*Fioretti*, Stigmata, II).

When therefore Francis left La Verna he was, in spite of his physical sufferings in a joyous mood, a mood that prevailed for the rest of his days.

It took them two months to reach the Porziuncola; the journey had to be taken, as we have seen, by short stages to lessen the discomfort for Francis. When he reached 'home', he insisted on making a preaching journey though he could no longer walk but had to ride an ass. This exertion proved too much for his weakened body; moreover his eyes were causing much pain and the sight was failing. It so happened that Pope Honorius had temporarily left Rome as a result of local tumults and had come to Rieti. Cardinal Ugolino was with him, and as soon as he heard of Francis's affliction, he told the friars to bring him to Rieti so that the papal physicians could examine him. Thomas of Celano has an interesting note on the relations between the Cardinal and Francis.

'For his part he burned with exceeding love toward the holy man and therefore whatever the blessed man said or did pleased him, and he was often deeply stirred by the mere sight of him. He himself bears witness that however disturbed or vexed he might be, on seeing Francis and talking with him all mental clouds were dispersed, serenity returned, melancholy was put to flight and joy breathed on him from above. He ministered to Francis as a servant to his lord. (*Celano*, I. para. 101).

Brother Elias was unremitting in his care of Francis, who was comforted by having with him five of his most faithful companions: Bernard of Quintaville, Leo, Angelo, Ruffino and Masseo. When the last three had arranged for some 'good religious' to establish a friary at La Verna, they came south to rejoin their leader. Two 'good religious' had been sent there by Francis from Monte Casale.

Francis asked his companions to halt at San Damiano on the way to Rieti, but he was suddenly taken so much worse that it was impossible to continue the journey for the time. Sister Clare had a hut constructed in the little garden, and there Francis was sheltered. He was patient under his sufferings though a plague of mice added to his discomfort. Yet the joyous mood did not desert him, and it was then that he composed his Praise of Created Things, or the Canticle of the Sun, as it is best known. It is the earliest extant poem in Italian;

Most High, Omnipotent, Good Lord,
Thine be the praise, the glory, the honour and all benediction.
To Thee alone, Most High, they are due, and no man is
worthy to mention Thee.

Be Thou praised, my Lord, with all Thy creatures,
above all Brother Sun,
who gives the day and lightens us therewith.

And he is beautiful and radiant with great splendour,
of Thee, Most High, he bears similitude.

Be Thou praised, my Lord, of Sister Moon and the stars,
in the heaven hast Thou formed them, clear and precious and
comely.

Be Thou praised, my Lord, of Brother Wind,
and of the air, and the cloud, and of fair and all weather,
by the which Thou givest to Thy creatures sustenance.

Be Thou praised, my Lord, of Sister Water,
   which is much useful and humble and precious and pure.

Be Thou praised, my Lord, of Brother Fire,
   by which Thou hast lightened the night,
and he is beautiful and joyful and robust and strong.

Be Thou praised, my Lord, of our Sister Mother Earth,
   which sustains and hath us in rule,
    and produces divers fruits with coloured flowers and herbs.

It is a little surprising that Francis did not call on the beasts and birds to praise God.

While Francis was at San Damiano a bitter feud broke out between the Bishop and the Commune, so bitter that the Bishop excommunicated the magistrates. When Francis heard this, he summoned Brother Pacifico who has been called the poet laureate of the early Fratres Minores; to him Francis explained what he had in mind. A brother was sent off to gather the magistrates together in the bishop's palace, and, such was the prestige of Francis, they assembled there and were met by Brother Pacifico and some of the brethren. They then sang Francis's new Canticle to which he had added these two verses;

Be Thou praised, my Lord, of those who pardon for Thy love
   and endure sickness and tribulations.

Blessed are they who will endure it in peace,
   for by Thee, Most High, they shall be crowned.[1]

The Bishop and the magistrates, were deeply affected and they made their peace. Francis was so encouraged at the outcome of his intervention, that he sent Brother Pacifico with some compansions, 'God's gleemen', to preach and sing wherever they went. After the sermon, the friars were to sing the Canticle, and then to say, 'We are the minstrels of the

---

[1]This translation was made by Robert Steele (*Speculum Perfectionis*, CXX).

Lord, and for these things we wish to be paid by you, that is, that you should remain in true penitence'.

After some weeks at San Damiano, Francis was able to travel again by short stages to Rieti where he was lodged in the bishop's palace, but, the papal court meant not only overcrowding but constant going to and fro; all this bustle was too much for the sick man, so he was taken to one of his favourite retreats, Fonte Colombo. It was there that the papal physicians applied their remedies which, to us, seem more tormenting than the disease itself. The first means used was to cauterize the temples. As the iron was being heated, Francis exclaimed, 'O Brother Fire, among all creatures, God has made you noble and useful to men. Be gentle with me, for I have always loved you, and always will, for the love of him who made you!' He bore the intense pain without flinching. Further remedies were tried; a vein was opened above each ear, then each was pierced with a red-hot iron. All this unavailing torture could only have served to shorten the sufferer's life. Cardinal Ugolino had not given up hope. He persuaded the brethren to take Francis to an eminent physician in Siena. There, and indeed throughout these wearisome journeys, Francis was received with great reverence; there were rumours of the stigmata. Many came to seek his blessing or hoping to have their ills cured. The physician was not able to help him.

Francis had a serious hemorrhage one night; the brethren were greatly alarmed as he seemed at the point of death. In their grief they exclaimed, 'Father, what shall we do without you — sheep without a shepherd?' When Francis had sufficiently recovered, he called to him Brother Benedict of Pirato, the priest who celebrated Mass daily in the sick room. To him, Francis said,

'Write how I bless my brethren who are in the Order, and who shall come unto the end of the world. And since on account of my weakness and the pain of my infirmity I may not speak, in these three words I make plain my will and intention briefly to all my brethren, present and to come: namely, that in token of my memory and benediction and will, they should always love one another like as I have loved and do love them; and that they should always love and observe our Lady Poverty, and always remain faithful subjects to the prelates and clergy of holy Mother Church.' (*Speculum Perfectionis,* LXXXVIII).

The brethren sent word to Brother Elias who hurried to Siena and arranged to remove Francis to the Porziuncola, a decision that must have rejoiced the sufferer. To appreciate what followed it should be borne in mind how prominent a place the relics of saints had in medieval religion. There was what we should regard as an unseemly, if not superstitious, belief in the efficacy of the saints in safeguarding places and people. The most unscrupulous means, including robbery, were used to get relics. Elias was well aware of this and he knew that there would be fierce competition to get possession of the body of Francis who was popularly recognised as a saint in the last years of his life. The leading contenders would be the Perugians. The precautions he took, however, must not be thought of solely as a sign of worldly considerations as to what would happen after Francis's death. There can be no doubt that Elias had a deep affection and reverence for his leader and every possible (and some impossible)means were used to lessen his sufferings and prolong his life. Indeed, it was providential that the Vicar-General at this time was a masterful man. So Elias decided that the return to the Porziuncola must be by unfrequented roads; a rest of a few days on this eighty mile journey was made at the Celle of Cortona when they were within range of Perugia. Elias sent to Assisi for a guard and an armed escort was sent. When they safely reached the city, the citizens refused to let them go farther; they insisted that the bishop's palace was a far more secure place than the Porziuncola where Francis so much wanted to go.

He would have liked to get to the Pentecost Chapter of that year, 1226, but he was too weak. So he dictated a letter to the assembled friars urging them to revere and honour the Body and Blood of Our Lord in the Blessed Sacrament, and warning those that were priests that they should always say Mass 'with a holy and clean intention.' He asked Buongiovanni, his physician, to say how long he had to live, and after some hedging, the doctor told him that death was not far off. Francis exclaimed, 'Welcome, Sister Death!' And he added these verses to his Canticle;

> *Be Thou praised, my Lord, of our Sister Bodily Death,*
> *from whom no man living may escape.*
> *Woe to those who die in mortal sin.*

> *Blessed are they who are found in Thy most holy will*
> *for the second death shall not work them ill.*

> *Praise ye and bless my Lord, and give Him thanks,*
> *and serve Him with great humility.*

Francis encouraged the brothers about him to sing his Canticle and he himself would sing it at night when he was wakeful. Elias ventured to remonstrate since the people were saying, 'Why does this man show such lightheartedness who is near death? He ought to be thinking of death.' To this Francis replied that he daily meditated on his end, and added, 'Suffer me, brother, to rejoice in the Lord, both in His praises and in my infirmities.' (*Speculum Perfectionis*, CXXI).

He had a relapse and it seemed that death was indeed at hand and the brethren begged for his blessing. Elias was seated at his left hand and the others were seated around.

'Francis crossed his hands, laid his right hand on Elias' head and said (he being deprived of the light and use of his

outward eyes), "On whom am I holding my right hand?"
"On Brother Elias," was the answer. "And that is my
wish," said he, adding, "I bless you, my son, in and
through all things, and as the Most High has in your
hands increased my brethren and sons, so also, over you
and in you do I bless them all. God, the King of all, bless
you in heaven and in earth. I bless you as I can, and more
than I can, and what I cannot may He who can do all
things do in you. God remember your work and toil, and
may a share be reserved for you in the recompense of the
just. May you find every blessing you desire, and may that
which you do worthily ask be fulfilled. Fare you well, all
you my sons in the fear of God and remain in Him always,
for a great trial is coming upon you and tribulation draws
nigh. Happy are they who shall persevere in the things
they have begun, for the scandals that are to be shall
separate some from them. But I am hastening to the
Lord,and am now confidently going to my God, whom in
my spirit I have served with devotion.' (*Celano*, I, para.
108).

Much can be read into that blessing, that was also a
prophecy. Did Francis in the clear light that comes to the
dying, see that the Order would soon be disrupted by
divergent interpretations of his teaching and example? Did he
select Elias for special consideration because he sensed the
dangerous tendencies that were at war in the personality of his
Vicar-General?

At last the Assisians were persuaded to allow Francis to be
taken 'with all speed to the "place" of the Porziuncola; for he
wished to give back his soul to God there where he first knew
the way of truth perfectly.' So with an armed guard and a
phalanx of citizens, they carried him in a litter down the steep
road to the plain. There he asked them to halt and to place
him so that his sightless eyes were turned towards Assisi.

Raising himself a little, he blessed the city of his birth.

'Lord, like as this city of old was, as I believe, a place and habitation of wicked men, so I see that on account of the abundance of thy mercy in the time which hath pleased Thee, Thou hast singularly shewn it the multitude of Thy mercies. On account of Thy goodness alone, Thou hast chosen it to Thyself that it might be the place and habitation of those who should know Thee in truth, and should give glory to Thy Holy Name, and should shew forth the odour of good fame, of holy life, of most true doctrine, and of Evangelical Perfection to all Christian People. I ask of Thee therefore, Oh Lord Jesus Christ, Father of mercies, that Thou shouldst not consider our ingratitude but be ever mindful of Thy most abundant pity which Thou hast shewn towards it, that it may ever be the place and habitation of those who know Thee truly, and glorify Thy most blessed and glorious Name, forever and ever, Amen.' (*Speculum Perfectionis*, CXXIV).

12.

'Welcome, Sister Death!'

IT was at the Porziuncola about Michaelmas that Francis dictated his Testament, which, he emphasised, was not another Rule, but 'a remembrance, admonition or exhortation.' He began by reviewing his own call to leave the world and 'live according to the form of the Holy Gospel.' He bade brothers 'fear, love and honour' priests and not to preach in parishes without the goodwill of the priests. Then he recalled their early way of life, how, 'those who came, gave to the poor all that they possessed and they were content with one tunic patched within and without, and with a cord and breeches, and we wished for nothing more.' The brethren should work with their hands or beg alms from door to door. Then came an admonition that clashed with the trend of opinion that so disturbed him when he noticed it among some of the Ministers and brethren.

'Let the brethren take care not on any account to receive churches, poor dwelling-places or any other things which are built for them, unless they be such as become the holy poverty which we have vowed in the Rule, always dwelling here as pilgrims and strangers. I strictly command all the brethren by obedience that wherever they may be, they shall not dare to ask any letter of the Roman Court, either themselves or by any intermediary person, neither for a church nor for any other place, nor under pretext of preaching, nor on account of bodily persecution; but wherever they are not received, let them flee into another land to do penance with the blessing of God.' (*Cuthbert*, P. 452).

At the same time he declared that he put himself under obedience to the Vicar-General 'because he is my master,' and he required all the brethren to submit to the Ministers as they were in duty bound to do. Here we can see elements of the conflicts that were to break out within a few years. The Testament ended with this blessing

> 'And whosoever shall observe these things let him be filled in heaven with the blessing of the Most High Father, and on earth with the blessing of His beloved Son, together with the Most Holy Spirit, the Paraclete, and all the Powers of heaven and all the saints. And I, Brother Francis, your little one and servant, in so far as I can, confirm unto you within and without this most holy blessing. Amen.' (*Cuthbert*, p. 454).

Sick people often have fancies for special foods, and Francis was no exception. At one time it was for parsley, at another a particular kind of fish, and then he recalled a sweetmeat (*mostacciolo*) that the Lady Giacoma used to prepare for him when he was in Rome. Does this craving for particular foods seem out of place? Francis was not an ascetic. His rule was that brothers should be content with whatever food they could beg, and, as we have seen, he gave one or two object lessons on this theme, but, except when fasting, his practice was to eat whatever was put before him. His was a sociable nature.

Francis had no sooner expressed a wish for some *mostacciolo* than the brothers were surprised by the arrival of the Lady Giacomo with her sons and attendants. There is no need to see anything supernatural in this coincidence. News of Francis's mortal sickness quickly spread and Elias would have kept Cardinal Ugolino informed; the Pope had at last been able to return to Rome. The lady's anxiety brought her to the Porziuncola though she must have thought she was approaching an armed camp; there was not only a strong guard mounted by the Assisian magistrates but there was a throng of people patiently waiting for news, or in the hope of seeing Francis. The brothers were at a non plus; no woman was allowed to put foot in the grounds of the Porziuncola; the last one to do so had been Sister Clare. Francis soon solved the problem; the rule, he said, did not apply to 'Brother' Giacomo as he called her. She brought with her some of the food he liked and also some grey cloth and other cloths suitable for his burial.

Sister Clare was also grieving at the thought of the loss of this beloved friend and she sent a message to Francis telling him of her distress. He dictated these words of comfort for her;

'I, little Brother Francis, desire to follow the life and poverty of our most high Lord Jesus Christ, and of His most holy mother, and to persevere therein until the end. And I beseech you, my ladies, and I give you counsel that you live always in this most holy life and poverty. And be greatly careful of yourselves lest by the teaching or counsel of any one, you in any way or at any time draw away from it (*Cuthbert,* p. 457).

As the end approached, he said to the brothers,

'See, my brothers, that you never leave this place: if you are thrust out on one side, enter it again on the other: for truly this place is holy and the dwelling of God. Here when we were but few, the Most High multiplied us; here with the light of His wisdom, he enlightened the hearts of His poor ones: here with the fire of His love, He set our wills on fire; here whosoever prays with a devout heart, will obtain what he asks and whoever offends will be harshly punished. Wherefore, O sons, hold this place of God's dwelling, worthy of all honour; and with all your heart in the voice of exultation and praise, confess to God therein.' (*Celano,* I, para. 106).

Then he bade them sing his Canticle and he himself recited

the Psalm, 'I cried to the Lord with my voice.' He asked a brother to read the twelfth chapter of St. John's Gospel. The last moments are best given in the words of Thomas of Celano.

'Then, for that he was about to become dust and ashes, he bade that he should be laid on sackcloth and sprinkled with ashes. All the brethren came together, and, as they stood reverently by and awaited his blessed departure and happy consummation, his most holy soul was released from the flesh and absorbed into the abyss of light, and his body fell asleep in the Lord.' (*Celano*, I. para. 110).

* * * * * *

Francis of Assisi died on the 4th October 1226, twenty years after his conversion and in his forty-fourth year. Early the next morning they carried his body from the Porziuncola to Assisi, but they paused at San Damiano so that Sister Clare and her community could venerate the stigmata. A sepulchre had already been prepared in San Giorgio where Francis had gone to school and where he had preached his first sermon. There he was laid to rest until a more permanent shrine could be erected.

It was on the 16th July 1228 that Cardinal Ugolino, now Pope Gregory IX, came to Assisi and solemnly pronounced the canonization of his old friend.

* * * * * *

Elias at once set about raising a great church in honour of the founder of the Fratres Minores. This is not the place to discuss the unhappy controversy that was aroused by Elias's ambitious plans. Four years after Francis's death the building of the basilica was sufficiently advanced for his body to be transferred, and the 5th May, 1230 was the momentous day for which so many had waited. There is no clear account of what happened. Elias was determined that there should be no possibility of the body being stolen. One story is that when the bearers reached the Lower Church, they alone were allowed in and Elias had the door shut and bolted to prevent the indignant magistrates and citizens from entering. He then had the body buried in a secret place. Another possibility is that he had had the body buried some days before. What is certain is that few knew of the burial place and none of them revealed where exactly the body was laid.

This strange action of Elias caused all kinds of rumours to circulate[1]. Was the body actually there? And so on. It was assumed, and rightly, that it was somewhere in the rocky foundations under the high altar of the Lower Church but its position was not certainly known. It was not until 1818 that a systematic search was carried out. Tunnels were driven into the foundations and at length the tomb was found; the saint's body was enshrined by closely fitted blocks of trevertine brought from the Roman wall of Assisi. The area was opened up and a crypt chapel formed round the burial place which was guarded by a heavy iron grill.

It was fitting that later on the remains of Brothers Leo, Angelo, Ruffino and Masseo were transferred to tombs cut in the wall of the apse behind the altar of St Francis.

* * * * * *

The Feast of St Francis of Assisi is celebrated on the 4th October, and that of the Imprinting of the Sacred Stigmata on the 17th September.

* * * * * *

FRANCIS, POOR AND HUMBLE, ENTERS HEAVEN A RICH MAN
AND HEAVENLY MUSIC DOES HIM HONOUR. ALLELUIA.

---

[1] How Elias managed all this is not known. A similar action followed the death of St Clare in 1253. Her body was placed in San Giorgio (as Francis's had been). This church was incorporated in the present Santa Chiara, but the exact place of her entombment was not discovered until 1850.

13.

Saint Francis of Assisi

ST Francis of Assisi captured the affection not only of his generation but of all generations since, both Catholic and Protestant. None of the other saints has won such universal esteem, an esteem that always has a touch of personal friendliness. The nearest parallel, perhaps, is St. Thomas More, 'a man for all seasons'. Both of them were so companionable, so human.

We associate St Francis with springtime; we think of him singing his way through the lovely valleys of Italy, rejoicing in the freshness of nature, the flowers, the woods and meadows and streams, the birds and beasts, and meeting folk of all kinds with a smile and the greeting, 'Good-morrow, good people, the Lord give you peace.' That, of course, is one side of the picture. He was also tramping the roads and clambering up mountain paths in rain and wind and storm and snow; sometimes soaked to the skin and having only an overshadowing rock as a shelter for the night; cold and hungry. But the idealised picture has this much of truth in it, for 'freshness' is a mark of the spirit and mission of Il Poverello. His own spiritual progress was unusual, and there was freshness in the kind of religious Order he founded.

As a youth he had been a gay companion, enjoying the lavish spending his father encouraged; there must have been a charm about his personality that brought him into a higher social circle than his family standing warranted. Yet there was no hint of licentiousness nor of concupiscence. The ideal he had set before himself, in part derived perhaps from the *Chansons de Geste,* was that of the 'perfect, gentle knight', who

'loved chivalry
Truth and honour, freedom and courtesy.'

And such indeed he became, for it remained as an ideal but raised to a higher level than that of social status or prowess in war. When Francis admitted Guy of Cortona to the Order, he said, 'Courtesy is one of the attributes of God ... and courtesy is the sister of charity.' The personal charm remained; this, his religious fervour and single-mindedness, captured popes, cardinals, bishops and priests as well as counts and knights and labouring men and women. It was difficult to say 'No' to Francis.

We have followed his lonely wrestling with his spiritual problems, for it was a lonely search since there is no record of his having sought anyone's advice; nor did he go to books for guidance; the Gospels gave him all he wanted. The words of Christ were henceforth his safeguard.

It is impossible to know all the influences that lead to a conversion, from 'this-worldly' to 'other-wordly', from a life of creaturely pleasure to a life dedicated to God. There must be a sub-conscious preparation and the nature of this eludes us. One factor in Francis's change of life was his recoil from his care-free, voluptious youth; yet what occasioned the revulsion is not known. It was this that led to his 'converse with Lady Poverty'. This is well put in the opening pages of the *Sacrum Commercium*.

'Wherefore the blessed Francis, as a true imitator and disciple of the Saviour, from the beginning of his conversion gave himself to the seeking out of holy Poverty to find her and to hold her, with all zeal, with all desire, with all determination, doubting nothing of the enemy, fearing nothing that was against him, shunning no toil, refusing no affliction of the body, so at the last his desire should be granted him to attain her to whom the Lord had given the keys of the Kingdom of Heaven.'

He came to have a horror of the tyranny of possessions and of the craving to own more and more things, that draw men away from the contemplation of Christ. Money, the use of which had meant so much to him as a youth, he came to despise and forbade his followers even to touch it. To quote Thomas of Celano (II, para. 80):

'The saint taught those coming to the Order previously to give a bill of divorcement to the world, by first offering outwardly their goods, and then inwardly themselves to God. He admitted to the Order none but those who expropriated themselves and were keeping back nothing at all, both because of the word of the Holy Gospel and lest they should cause scandal by retaining a treasure-chest.'

He ignored the practical difficulties that resulted from this fierce renunciation of possessions. He was not at first thinking of a vast number of men flocking into the Order; he was thinking of the dozen or so who came to join him in the early months. But even when numbers grew beyond all expectations, he still adhered to his original rule.

His 'converse with Lady Poverty' gave him an intense compassion for the poor and the sick, and he even envied anyone who seemed poorer than himself. As Thomas of Celano (II. para. 83). tells us:

'But whereas he had banished from himself all other envy, from the envy of poverty alone he could not free himself. If ever he saw one poorer than himself he envied that man forthwith and feared to be outdone by him in the contest for poverty.'

Francis must have seen himself, as in a mirror, in the Gospel story when Our Lord told the rich young man to sell all his possessions, give the proceeds to the poor and 'then come back and follow me.' Christ was not laying down a general injunction; he was speaking to the condition of that particular young man. So Francis, while exacting, some said obstinately, absolute poverty as a condition for entering the Order, did not lay it down as a rule for those living in the world; for them he wrote the most sensible letter of guidance that has ever been sent to the laity. The Third Order was the outcome.

Poverty was not an end in itself; for Francis complete freedom from earthly ties was a necessary condition for bringing the Gospel to the people, especially to the poor who would listen more eagerly to those as poor as themselves. So he himself renounced his inheritance and severed all connection with his family.

The love of things, of ownership was the sin of pride; to combat this the Christian must foster the virtue of humility. In the *Speculum Perfectionis* (LXIII) we read the following incident;

> 'When he went through the city of Assisi, a poor woman begged an alms of him for the love of God. And he immediately gave her the mantle which he had on his back and forthwith without delay he confessed in the presence of those who followed how he had thence vain glory. And we have seen and heard so many examples like to these of his great humility, we who were always in his company, that neither with words nor with letters can we narrate them.'

That suggests the pen of Brother Leo.

He overcame his pride in possessions, but he would have been inhuman not to have felt more than common satisfaction in the phenomenal popularity of his friars. Sometimes he would adopt extreme measures to subdue any sign of pride in his achievement. On one occasion he had himself dragged through Assisi, clad only in his breeches, with a rope round his neck. Such a spectacle was less startling in days when flagellants paraded the streets, than it would be today. It was an expression of Francis's urge to give visual expression to religious ideas; he knew that this was one way of making ordinary folk think and he counted any personal humiliation as a trifle if some soul could be saved. His contest with Brother Leo is another example of the constant struggle he had to subdue pride and win humility.

His preaching was based on the Gospel of repentance, remission of sins and change of life. Like the apostles, the friars 'went out and preached, bidding men to repent.' No sermon of his has been recorded but there are a few brief references that help to fill the gap. When Ruffino was ordered to go to Assisi and preach, Francis followed him and we are told:—

> 'Then Saint Francis went up into the pulpit, and began to preach so marvellously of the contempt of the world, of holy penitence, of voluntary poverty, and of the desire of the kingdom of heaven, and of the nakedness and shame of the passion of our Lord Jesus Christ, that all that heard the preaching, men and women in great multitude, began to weep most bitterly with devout and contrite hearts; and not there alone, but in all Assisi was there that day such weeping for the passion of Christ, that never had there been the like.'

There was a freshness in the way Francis formed the Fratres Minores. St. Augustine and St. Benedict and others had drawn up Rules that counted for every hour in the day of a monk or nun. Francis had no wish to bind the friars with such meticulous regulations, so his Rule was little more than a statement of general principles. The friar was left free to arrange the working out of his vocation; he could arrange his daily prayer and activities as he felt most profitable to his ministry. He could be a preacher, or a hermit, or live in a small community, and he could change from one to the other as the Holy Spirit directed. This complete trust was sometimes betrayed and Francis knew enough of the world and its temptations not to be surprised at failures. He saw too that some would wish to change the Order into a more disciplined body. One comment of his was in reply to a friar who complained that the original fervour was passing and some were

'counting for naught the way of holy simplicity, humility and poverty' ... the holy man answered and said to him: 'May the Lord have mercy on thee, brother, since thou wilt be contrary and adversary to me, and mix me up in those things which pertain not to my office. For as long as I had the office of prelacy over the friars, and they remained in their vocation and profession, though from the beginning of my conversion I was always infirm, yet with my small solicitude I satisfied them by example and preaching. But after I saw that the Lord multiplied the number of friars, and that they, on account of their luke-warmness and want of spirit, began to depart from the right and secure way by which they had been used to walk, and entering on the broader way which leads to death were not following their vocation and profession and a good example, nor did they wish to abandon that dangerous and deadly journey which they had begun for my preaching and admonition and the example which I showed them continually, therefore, I handed over the rule of the Order to the Lord Cardinal and the Ministers ... But since I am not able to correct and amend them by preaching, admonition and example, I will not become an executioner, punishing and flogging them, like the magistrates of this world.' (*Speculum Perfectionis*, LXXI).

It was providential that Francis laboured under two popes and two cardinals who were fully sympathetic. They believed in him though they had doubts how the idea of absolute poverty would work out in practice. They trusted him as a loyal son of the Church. The result justified that trust for the

Fratres Minores brought about a renewal of religion during the twelfth and thirteenth centuries. From time to time the Church has become too bureaucratic and sluggish and there is a need for spiritual renewal. Though impulse may die out in time and authoritarianism again take command something of value always remains. No one has equalled Saint Francis in the freshness and power of his impact on religious life, but, factious quarrels among the Franciscans brought their effective ministry almost to naught; they too had to experience renewal. Yet the influence of Francis has never been limited by the kind of institutionalism he so much disliked and distrusted. A vast multitude of people who have never met a friar owe much to the spirit and message of Saint Francis.

Spiritual life and influence cannot be measured and assessed; we can collect statistics of church attendance but only God knows if a man's presence in church has any true meaning. So too it is impossible to assess the religious value of all that the Franciscans have meant to the Church and the world. A Benedictine historian has written:

'The new life that Francis himself had lived and shown to others remained and remains in the Church, and has in all centuries inspired individuals and groups within his Order as the model for a type of sanctity which all recognize as Franciscan. It has, besides, enriched the spirit of all Europe, not only, or even principally, as a new manifestation of the brotherhood of all men and of the share of all creatures in the beauty and beneficence of God, but as a showing forth of the Gospel lived in its fullness with a detail and clarity rare to equal in any age, and as a revelation of the imitation of Christ crucified, in love and suffering, which though present in essence in all Christian sanctity, appeared in Francis in a new form to which the growing mind of Europe responded at once, and which was to prove the prototype of much which was to come in the religious life of the West.'[1]

[1] Dom David Knowles. *The Religious Orders in England*. Vol. 1 (1948) p. 126.

Appendix I

The Secular Franciscan Order

THE Secular Franciscan Order was called the Order of Penance, meaning Conversion to the Gospel; and generally it has until recently been called the THIRD ORDER, following the First Order of Religious Men in vows of Poverty, Chastity and Obedience and the Second Order — Sisters of Saint Clare, Poor Clares, in a vowed contemplative community life. Many other Franciscan Communities profess the Third Order RULE with a profession of the three Canonical Religious vows. Since all these are religious according to Church Law it has been decided to emphasise that Married and single laity without religious vows are not religious, but secular, though pertaining to the Franciscan Community. This change was officially made by Pope Paul VI in 1978 with the reform of the Rule. This emphasis was also meant to take development a great step further — namely, to reveal the Secular Order as an autonomous body in the Franciscan Community, and not a pious sociality organised and governed by the Friars. The new Rule reflects our developing understanding of what a Rule should be, a WAY OF LIFE, and not simply a long list of useful ascetical practices, rather negative in expression, concerned with unworldliness rather than with living in the world and living it as witnesses.

The whole inspiration of Francis that brought about such a reality as a Third Order is still quite valid and effective, though in eight centuries it has also needed its *aggiornamento.* Times have changed, the world has changed; a so-called Christian Europe has vanished; the Church herself has been discerning how better she may respond to the world through the Gospel. But in all that change the Church still returns to the importance of the Laity — the absolutely vital and necessary presence of every man and woman for the realisation of the Kingdom. Francis began as a layman — and for him layman never meant second class Christian. He intended to share his brotherhood with the laity. The Church confirmed this breakthrough — laity not having to swear oaths to fight for their noble Lord; not carrying arms; being a movement of Peace; not needing the cloister to be sure of their eternal salvation.

The layman is still invited to join the Franciscan Family in the secular order, approved by the Church. He must come to commit himself gradually through preparation, novitiate and profession of the Rule of Life. Sometimes the process has been publicised as an *easy* way, unfortunately; but the ideal is still Francis — and you cannot talk about easiness when you talk of his Christ-like love. It will always run the risk of attracting people who only want a devotional aid in their spiritual life — there will be a risk that the individual may never see anything more than that in it. But if it is the call of the Holy Spirit to draw closer to Christ, to commit yourself to the Gospel, then it must be a profession demanding growth in fidelity in growing poverty and obedience in the Spirit of Francis.

For the sake of information we can usefully adopt a summary of the Rule or WAY OF LIFE of the Secular Franciscan Order in the sixteen central articles as presented by Fr. Mariona Habig OFM.

The New Rule in a Nutshell

Sixteen Points to Remember by Fr. Marion A Habig O.F.M.

1. Follow the example of Saint Francis of Assisi, who made Christ the inspiration and the centre of his life with God and people.

2. Seek to encounter the living and active person of Christ in your brothers and sisters, in Sacred Scripture, in the Church, and in liturgical activity.

3. Go forth as witnesses and instruments of the Church's mission among all people, proclaiming Christ by your life and words.

4. Conform your thoughts and deeds to those of Christ by means of that radical interior change which the gospel itself calls "conversion."

5. Join in liturgical prayer in one of the forms proposed by the Church, reliving the mysteries of the life of Christ.

6. Express your ardent love for the Virgin Mary by imitating her complete self-giving and by praying earnestly and confidently.

7. Faithfully fulfil the duties proper to your circumstance of life, even in difficulties and persecutions.

8. Seek a proper spirit of detachment from temporal goods by simplifying your own material needs, and purify your hearts from every tendency and yearning for possession and power.

9. Acquire purity of heart because of the vocation you have embraced, and set yourselves free to love God and your brothers and sisters.

10. Accept all people as a gift of the Lord, and strive to create for the lowly conditions of life worthy of people redeemed by Christ.

11. Together with all people of good will, build a more fraternal and evangelical world so that the kingdom of God may be brought about more effectively.

12. Be in the forefront in promoting justice by the testimony of your human lives and your courageous initiatives.

13. Esteem work both as a gift and as a sharing in the creation, redemption, and service of the human community.

14. In your family cultivate the Franciscan spirit of peace, fidelity, and respect for life striving to make of it a sign of a world already renewed in Christ.

15. Respect all creatures, animate and inanimate, and strive to move from the temptation of exploiting creation to the Franciscan concept of universal kinship.

16. Seek out ways of unity and fraternal harmony through dialogue, and strive to bring joy and hope to others.

Further information can be obtained from any Franciscan community of Friars Minor, Or Friars Minor Capuchin, or Friars Minor Conventual.

To get in touch with the nearest community an enquiry in the first place can be sent to: THE REV. NATIONAL ASSISTANT S.F.O., Franciscan Friary, St. Antony's Road, Forest Gate, London E7 9QB.

Appendix II

One Thing More

Meditations on the Franciscan Vocation
by Brother Reginald, S.S.F.

FIRST MEDITATION

I COME from God. I belong to God. I go to God. If I think of myself in perspective, it must be in relation to God. Human nature, human life is meaningless apart from God.

I come from God. I belong to God. God made me, cares for me, knows me. The Lady Julian of Norwich had a vision. She saw a little thing the size of a hazel nut, lying in the palm of her hand. She was told: "This is everything that is made". But it was so small she wondered how it could exist. And she was told: "It lasts, and shall last for ever, because God loves it" She saw God "the Maker, the Keeper, the Lover".*

I cannot live apart from God, or be myself — my best — apart from him. I come from God: I belong to God. That's how things are and I've no choice in the matter. But I *go* to God: that's different. I'm made in God's image and meant to find my full stature in him, growing in response to his love. It's up to me whether I do or not. I belong — but I must choose whether I will live as one who belongs to God.

Jesus called men to follow him. "You did not choose me: I chose you". (John 15:16). We too are called to follow. We are friars because we believe God has called us to follow Christ in a particular way. Our life is a response. It all depends on His

---

*Julian of Norwich: *"Revelations of Divine Love"*, Chapter 5. Published by Anthony Clarke.

call. But we can only follow if we choose to.

Read Mark 10:17-22, a passage specially associated with the religious life. The rich young man (Matthew 19:22 — he reminds us of St. Francis) asked Jesus what he must do to receive eternal life — to live fully and in the best possible way. When Jesus said "You know the commandments", he replied, "Yes: all my life I have kept them". Then Jesus looked at him with love and challenged him. "One thing more is necessary for you. Sell all you have ... then come and follow me". The man went away sad, for he was rich.

For *him* there was a special calling — one thing more which the Lord asked. Whether in the end he took this costly step we do not know. But we do know that *Jesus loved him and left him free to make his own decision.*

Our vocation is to do the extra thing Jesus asks. Eternal life — real fellowship with God — means to hear and answer his call. His call is always a call to *give ourselves*. Becoming a novice means a readiness to hear his call and to accept the religious life if God makes it clear to us that this is what he wants — that this "one thing extra" is for me.

Give thanks to God for creating you and calling and leading you thus far (see the General Thanksgiving in the Book of Common Prayer): Help me, Lord, to listen and to answer your call. Help me to be faithful to the choice I have made and to follow all the way where you will lead. Show me the way and give me strength to persevere day by day.

SECOND MEDITATION

It used to be the custom, when a man was clothed as a novice in the Society of Saint Francis, for him to ask "for the mercy of God and the religous life and habit". The friars no longer use this form of words, but it was a useful reminder to us that the religious life and habit go together. We do not wear the habit because it's attractive and makes people notice us. New clothes do not alter the man inside them. But our habit is meant to be a symbol of a new kind of life.

In early days it was the custom to put a white robe upon every newly baptized Christian. This was the sign of the new life they had in Christ. We put on the character of Christ, like a new garment: Romans 13:14; Galatians 3:27. A religious is called first to be a faithful Christian — to have the character of Christ. We recall that some of the early friars spoke of Francis as "the mirror of perfection". Every Christian is called to be that. But what poor mirrors we are. How hard to see in us the reflection of Christ.

The new character is *given* to us. it is not something we have naturally or can acquire on our own. See Philippians 3:9. The new character, like the righteousness of Christ, is God's gift which we receive in faith. it is not like a tailor-made garment, fitting us as we are now, but like a suit made for a growing child; it is too big for him and he has to grow into it. We can think of the Christian life as growing into the measure of Christ's character (Ephesians 4:13). We can think of the religious life as a process of growing. We must keep on growing until we fit the habit and all that it means.

The process of growing is the work of the Holy Spirit who forms Christ in us. But he does not force us and we have day by day to make the choice to follow and to use the grace we are given.

Read Philippians 3:9-14 and Galatians 6:15. Christ makes us new creatures. But we must keep our will, our desire, fixed on him who is the goal. In fact, we have not reached the goal, but fall short of it. The only way in which we can let our Lord renew us is through penitence. We are sinners. Never can we say we have reached perfection and be satisfied with ourselves, but only "God be merciful to me ..." (Luke 18:9-14). Penitence means turning to God, without boasting or pretence, but *just as we are.* We turn to him in faith and hope. We know he forgives, and forgiveness means the restoration of our relationship with God. Forgiveness is the constant way of renewal.

So we are clothed with the robe of righteousness, the character of Christ. We read in the old "Legend of St. Clare" that the saint took "the habit of penitence". Our habit — our character — must be that of penitence. In the Old Testament sackcloth is the mark of penitence. A beautiful tapestry is woven on sackcloth or canvas. When it is completed you cannot see the canvas, but it is there — the base on which something beautiful has to be worked and without which there would be no tapestry. So penitence is the foundation of our spiritual growth — the canvas on which the Holy Spirit can work the tapestry which will become the image and character of Christ in us.

Lord, may I know you, and may I know myself. Since in the light of Christ I see my sin and my need, may his forgiving grace lift me up, and keep me faithful day by day.

THIRD MEDITATION

When Francis gave up his wealth and fine clothes and left his home to follow Jesus as a poor man, he walked out of the city dressed in a rough sackcloth tunic on the front of which he chalked a large cross. This was the sign that he belonged to Jesus and was committed to his service. He went off singing. The way he had chosen — to follow Christ in the way of the cross — was the way of freedom and joy. This freedom did not mean doing just as he liked, but being free from self and free to serve God; free to obey Christ and so to be himself.

All Christians are marked with the cross in baptism. The cross made invisibly on our foreheads is meant to become visible in our lives and characters.

With the religious habit goes the girdle, a sign that we are bound to Christ. At his profession, a Franciscan brother stands with his arms stretched out in the form of a cross while he receives the girdle and the minister says; "As you are bound to Christ so in him you are free".

The way of the cross is the way of humility and obedience. See John 4:34 and Philippians 2:5-9. It is the way of glory and salvation, not something wasteful, negative and shameful.

Obedience is the mark of the Christian family; Mark 3:31-35; Matthew 21:28-31. We are, says St. Paul, to have the mind of Christ; Philippians 2:5. Humility is the mark of the Franciscan life, and until a man has learnt it he will find obedience irksome and an affront to his freedom. But it is in fact the way we have chosen and way of *true* freedom.

THE VOW OF OBEDIENCE

1. It binds us to Christ. But we take it freely. Though very often we shall not like it, we have to learn to understand and appreciate it as "the vow of freedom".†

2. What really worries us is not the humiliation of obedience but the knowledge that we are not truly free. We are so constantly slaves to our moods, prejudices, instincts and pride. So we are not ready to do the things we don't like doing. We are not free always to recognize Christ and serve him in other people, and, therefore,not ready to forgive or ask forgiveness. In the religious life we are called to witness to the sovereignty of God in a world where men are slaves to their instincts and emotions and where so much hatred, cruelty and unhappiness come from our human limitations and our pride. We are called to show in a special way that the baptismal vow of renunciation is a positive bid for freedom. By the power of the Holy Spirit we are made strong and enabled to become masters of ourselves; bound to Christ the Master,but truly free.

†Sister Edna Mary, Dss.C.S.A., *The Religious Life* (London, 1968), 164ff.

Obedience is the love given by somebody who is free to give it. See John 14:23-26.

3. We are called to a life in community in which we discover God's will for us. But our obedience does not mean simply doing without question what superiors tell us. Our obedience is grounded in humility and respect for one another. It means freely exercising our initiative and responsibility for the good of others. It means an openness to each other, a readiness to explain and apologize. It springs from that trust of our brothers which is the basis of our family life.

Charles de Foucauld said that "Jesus is the master of the impossible".* He can change us, make us new, and set us free to become Christ to others. Père Voillaume wrote to the Little Brothers of Jesus that none of our life in religion "can be real and genuine unless our hearts are changed and become humble, freed of self-love, surrendered beyond question to the love of Jesus crucified. And that is the work of a lifetime, a work to begin again each morning".‡

Lord, pour into my heart and into the hearts of all men everywhere, the Spirit of our Lord Jesus Christ, that by his Spirit we may be changed and made new.

FOURTH MEDITATION

Many Christians think of the religious life as something negative and restricted. They have forgotten their own baptismal vows. Already we have thought of the baptismal vow of renunciation (or world, flesh, and devil) as an assertion of freedom; to renounce something is to refuse to be a slave to it, but rather to have it under control.

*Quoted in R. Voillaume: *Seeds of the Desert* (Published by Anthony Clarke, England, 1955, 1973), **124.**
‡R. Voillaume: op. cit., **99,** 1973.

Our religious life and vows say in a particular way what the baptismal vows say, ie., that God comes first. Things we can possess, sex and self-will are not the top things. They belong to God and are only rightly used as they are given, consecrated to His service. The religious life means giving ourselves to God — not just giving up, but giving back to God what belongs to Him.

POVERTY, OR SIMPLICITY

The rich young man (see Mark 10:17-22 again, and Matthew 19:16-30) was told he needed one thing extra. It was to sell all he had and give to the poor — "and you will have treasure in heaven". He reminds us of St. Francis who threw aside his wealth and the comforts of home and possessions in order to follow Christ in simplicity.

The idea of poverty is difficult. Br. Douglas, who founded the Society of Saint Francis in England, was acutely aware of the squalor and distress of the really poor. He wondered whether the brothers could ever speak of their own poverty. He preferred to speak of "simple living". What does our poverty mean?

1. It is the recognition of the value and goodness of everything that God has made. It is a reverence for creation which leads men to use all things responsibly, not selfishly or carelessly. It means a great concern about the world and about hunger, war, pollution and waste — about the evils which result from man's manipulation of God's world.

2. At his profession each Franciscan brother is bidden: "From now on call nothing your own". Our vow of poverty means being detached, being prepared and able to do without the things we think we need. So it expresses our dependence upon God.

3. Poverty does not mean literally having nothing. It does not mean squalor and destitution. Poverty as such is ugly, and people who are hungry and deprived of many necessities of life are in danger of being bitter and in despair. Such poverty degrades men and takes away their human dignity, and Christians have always fought this kind of poverty. Our voluntary poverty recognizes, on the other hand, the danger of wealth — the danger of forgetting God, and of relying on money and possessions and of putting them in God's place.

4. We need things and are allowed the use of them, for our work and study; we are allowed clothes and so on. What we have we share. We violate the spirit of poverty by being so attached to things that we are unwilling to part with them or do without them, and by not looking after the things we do have. Poverty is the responsibility of every brother in a house. So it is important to ask: am I prepared to go without — would I be prepared if necessary — anything I specially like (smoking, extra odd cups of coffee — lots of small things which I may discover have become quite important to me)?

5. It's not only a matter of money and possessions. We must share our talents, our abilities and our time. Simplicity means being detached from any of those things which cause division and jealousy. It means being detached from particular jobs and spheres of influence. While we must take trouble and try to do every job well, we must not guard any job so jealously that we can never give it up or allow somebody else to share in it. Our concern is with Christ and the reality of his kingdom — his rule — in this world, and not with our own importance.

6. It is the "vow of gratitude".* My whole life, my use of any

*Sister Edna Mary: *op. Cit.*, 133ff.

of God's creatures, should express praise and gratitude to the Creator. A mark of the Franciscan life is the joyful appreciation of all that God has made: "Praised be my Lord by all his creatures". See Colossians 3:17; 1 Corinthians 10:31; 11 Corinthians 8:9.

Here is a way of sharing the cross and a way of freedom. It guards our humility (our dependence upon God and upon each other) and our love.

God, by the life of blessed Francis you moved your people to a love of simple things. May we, after his example, hold lightly to the things of this world and store up for ourselves treasure in heaven: through Jesus Christ our Lord.

FIFTH MEDITATION

Francis, praying before the crucifix in the ruined church of San Damiano outside Assisi, heard Christ speaking to him, "Francis, build my church". Ready to obey, he began to repair the little church. But he gradually discovered that his work was not to build with stones. The church is made of "living stones" (1 Peter 2:5). It is the people of God. Francis was called to bring new life and hope to the church of his day through a brotherhood — an order — consecrated to obeying the holy gospel and serving God's people.

We hear the Lord's word to Francis today: "Build my church". It comes to us. We are called by the life of our community, our brotherhood, to be a means by which the Lord can give life to his church today and keep it in repair.

In a world where there are so many factors which keep people apart from each other — race, culture, temperament, political and business interests, possessions, and above all pride and sin (our unwillingness to understand and care for one another) — we are called by our community life to bear witness to the love of God. "Man was formed in the image of the blessed Trinity ... a man who is so self-contained as not to be bound to the sympathies of society round him is violating the law of his own being".* We are called to live as brothers and to care about people.

The religious life means being oneself, being fully human, not less than human. Our life in community is a reflection in miniature of the life of the church; it is a witness to the glory and potential of mankind, made in the image of God, the Holy Trinity.

Read John 15:1-10. Jesus gives us the picture of himself and his disciples, the picture of his church. As the branches are all nourished by the sap from the vine, so Christians are all fed with the same life. We are blood relations! What a thought for all of us who want to be independent and go our own way! But that's it; we have the life of the crucified, risen Christ within us — a powerful force of love which can break down the barriers of race, class, status, etc. This is something we have to begin to live out in our community.

Our Society is a family, We *join* the family. It's already there. But apart from the brothers there is no community. Each of us is equally responsible for making and maintaining the family.

THE VOW OF CHASTITY

This vow is often criticized and misunderstood as a negative thing. How wrong and stupid to think of crushing the emotions. Chastity means consecrating — offering to God and therefore disciplining — our emotions and our capacity to love. If you try to stamp them out, there's nothing left to give to God!

*R. M. Benson: *Instructions on the Religious Life* - Second Series (London, 1935), **19**

1. The vow of chastity, the vow of loving† means that human relations, affection and friendship are consecrated and enriched.

2. It means delighting in people, and in the privilege of being brothers and of meeting and ministering to other people. Thank God for people.

3. Like the vow of poverty it warns us against wanting to grasp and possess. We can possess and manipulate people for our own ends as we would things. Relationships go wrong when we are selfish and think of others as there mainly for our enjoyment and satisfaction. Chastity means detachment — delighting in and appreciating other people but not wanting to possess them or dominate. It means a disciplined love which springs from a reverence and respect for people.

    It is our vocation and ministry to help others to discover in themselves the dignity of the divine image. Jesus (Mark 10:21) loved the young man, but left him free to make his own decision. So a consecrated love always respects the dignity of the other person and leaves him free.

4. Love is the means by which the family, the community, the church, the kingdom are built. It is costly for it is the way of the cross. It is in relationships that we shall often experience the pain of the cross, the cost of discipleship. To be persevering and faithful in intercession; to try to widen the scope of our prayer and not let it be limited by our likes and dislikes; not to fret if work takes us away from those we particularly like — here are some tests of a disciplined and consecrated love.

5. Our relationships must be seen in terms of the vine and the branches. Every single branch is important. Each one

†Cp. Sister Edna Mary: *op cit.*, 149ff.

matters. But there's trouble brewing if the Christian cannot see the vine because of the branches.

To love is to *seek Christ* and to look for *him* in the people we meet. It is to look beyond the person to him in whose image he is made. To abide in Christ is the only safeguard of true love. The crucified, risen Lord makes him home in us; that is the secret. It is the Holy Spirit's work. The fruit of the Spirit (Galatians 5:22f) is a salad, all the ingredients of which are various expressions of love. They are the foundation of community!

Lord, make me an instrument of your peace!
Where there is hatred, let me sow love;
Where there is injury, pardon;
Where there is discord, union;
Where there is doubt, faith;
Where there is darkness, light;
Where there is sadness, joy.

O divine Master, grant that I may not so much seek To be consoled as to console,
To be understood as to understand,
To be loved as to love;
For it is in giving that we receive,
It is in forgiving that we are pardoned
And it is in dying that we are born to eternal life.

SIXTH MEDITATION

Jesus sent the apostles out with the message: "The kingdom of heaven is near" (Matthew 10:7). We have thought of the call of Christ and of the way of penitence, obedience, simplicity and love in which he asks us to follow him. This way of life is meant to help people to see and know that the kingdom of heaven is near.

Read John 1:43-51 (especially 51) and compare Genesis

28:10-17. Nathanael was told that his meeting with Jesus would lead to an experience he had never dreamed of. Here is an echo of Jacob's dream. Jacob awoke and could say that the place where he was was "the gate of heaven". Because Jesus has become man and shared our life and our dying, because he has risen and ascended to glory and sent his Spirit upon his people to make his presence real to them, heaven is open to us. Angels are going up and down the ladder set up between heaven and earth. Any place can be for us the Gate of Heaven.

This mystery (or reality) is represented in the eucharist. We are there "with angels ... and with the church in heaven and on earth", and heaven is open to us. We are "citizens of heaven" now (Philippians 3:20). Yet we know that we have not arrived. God's gift of eternal life is like a seed that grows. The eucharist is the sacrament of growth — spiritual food in the strength of which we are growing, and the constant source of new life in us. It looks ahead, towards the completion of the process. See John 6:53-58. The goal is not distant and irrelevant. It is Christ and the maturity of his manhood.

So we look towards heaven, yet here and now we share the life of heaven. "The kingdom of heaven is at hand".

Our corporate prayer lifts us to heaven and brings heaven to earth. This happens sacramentally in the eucharist. It is a mystery, i.e., what God does, not something we bring about. But it is not magic. The eucharist and the office go together. The office is basically scripture — reading the word of God and meditating on it. It represents our search for God, our desire for Him. In it we look at Christ. It sets our hearts on that goal toward which the sacrament enables us to grow.

Personal prayer as well as liturgical prayer are part of our rule. The very word office (*officium* = duty) reminds us that *prayer is our job*. In SSF our rule binds us to an hour's prayer daily in addition to the eucharist and the office.

The religious life is a witness that the kingdom of heaven is near. Our life, our ministry of service, should bear witness to it. But our life is not only "activity" — the kind of things people can see us doing and applaud. Prayer is equally part of our life and ministry, no less essential because it is hidden.

Any kind of work can sometimes become irksome and distasteful. That may happen without prayer. But we are called to follow our Lord in the way of the cross, and it should not surprise us if prayer is sometimes difficult.

Prayer is the means by which we put ourselves at God's disposal and let the Holy Spirit stretch us, as it were, so that we grow into our full stature as Christians (Ephesians 4:13). In prayer we are being drawn outside and beyond ourselves. We can be sure that in prayer — in adoration, penitence and intercession — we shall find the marks of the cross.

Prayer is —

1. what Christ does in us through the Holy Spirit. We should try to be quiet and relaxed and let him take charge. Prayer is an act of faith.

But prayer is —

2. our response to what God does, a response of our whole being. It is not inactivity, a state in which God, as it were, takes hold of us and pushes us about without our co-operation. Prayer is in fact our desire for God, and involves our wills — "faith working through love". (Galatians 5:6)

Charles de Foucauld kept in his chapel as focal points for his own prayer the reserved sacrament and the bible. They represented to him the ways in which Jesus came to him day by day. They also represented two elements in his prayer which were kept in balance, the sacramental (stillness and receptivity on the one hand) and the biblical (the mental activity and striving on the other).* It is right that we should try to keep this balance in our spiritual lives. Eucharist and bible were both important to St. Francis. It will always help us to guard against any possible waste or misuse of our prayer time, to have the bible open. Even if we don't think great thoughts we can try to keep our eyes on Jesus and hear his words.

If we are to be citizens of heaven and proclaim in our own persons and in our community the nearness of the kingdom, we must all be men of prayer — not necessarily good at it (for how can we tell?) but faithful in prayer. Remember that the place where we are struggling in darkness is the gate of heaven, wherever it may be.

We are asked to be faithful and to persevere, and we are promised not success but eternal life (Matthew 10:22b). After the war in Korea when the Christians could not tell what the future would bring and how the church would survive, they encouraged each other with this motto: "Endurance *is* Victory".

> *Thanks be to you, my Lord Jesus Christ,*
> *for all the benefits you have given me,*
> *for all the pains and insults you have borne for me.*
> *Most merciful redeemer, friend and brother,*
> *May I know you more clearly,*
> *Love you more dearly and*
> *Follow you more nearly, day by day.*
> *(St. Richard of Chichester)*

---

*R. Voillaume: *op. cit.*, **10,** 126. "Brother Charles would not only sit at Jesus' feet in the eucharist and keep his eyes fixed upon him in silence; he also always meditated on his words in the Gospel, so as to keep his life in tune with them" (*Ibid.*, **126**).